BUILDERS of the NATION

Helen S. Konz

TO SOW THE FALLOW SOIL

Winston-Derek Publishers, Inc.
Pennywell Drive P.O. Box 90883
Nashville, Tennessee 37209

First printing

Cover art: Stephen Konz

PUBLISHED BY WINSTON-DEREK PUBLISHERS, INC.
Nashville, Tennessee 37205

Library of Congress Catalog Card No: 92-85407
ISBN: 1-55523-556-5

Printed in the United States of America

Dedicated to my parents who nurtured me,
my children who inspired me,
and most of all to my husband
who supported and encouraged me.

Contents

I

The Experiment

The boy in front of the warehouse pulled the brocade lapels of his wool jacket close around his neck for protection from the cold, damp wind that blew strands of hair out of his neat queue. Curiously, he watched the ships with their sails furled to the high masts at the Liverpool wharves being loaded with bales of cloth, iron tools, chains, and casks of rum. Stevedores were unloading another ship of its cargo of raw sugar. He was unaware that the cloth and rum would buy slaves from Africa who would be taken in chains to the West Indies to work the plantations that produced the much desired sugar. How thrilling the life of a sailor must be, he thought, full of new sights and experiences! Spotting an opening in the long train of oxcarts that continued to bring cargo, he scampered across Wharf Road to get a closer look from a spot near a piling beside the dock. He could see through the late morning fog other ships in the Mersey River waiting to dock at the teeming port.

What an adventure it would be to board one of those ships and set sail for some distant port—Lisbon, maybe the Far East, Bombay, Shanghai, or maybe the New World! He had heard of Boston, Philadelphia, New York, and the new town named after Richmond on the Thames where the Virgin Queen Elizabeth I died.

So absorbed was he in his fantasy that he did not hear approaching footsteps. The greeting, "Good morning, lad," brought him sharply back to reality. "Interested in ships, are you?" the man asked.

"Oh, yes, indeed. I am fascinated by them . . . sir." The last was added as he turned to look fully at the stranger and sensed in his demeanor and apparel that here was a person of some importance. "Are you going to sail on one of them?"

"Definitely. My ship is there to your right. She's small, but sturdy and seaworthy, and I don't share her with any partners. When I finish inspecting her, she'll be ready to go."

"Where will she be sailing?" The boy was pleased with himself to have used the nautical "she."

"To the New World, lad,—a town called Richmond, in Virginia, the fairest colony on the coast. We'll be carrying tea, cloth, and tools mostly, and bringing back tobacco, furs, maybe some cotton. Would you like to come aboard and see the workings of a ship?" The captain's piercing gray eyes were captivating and created a surge of excitement in the boy.

"Oh yes, yes. Would it be all right?" he responded eagerly.

"Aye, it's certainly all right with me. I'm the captain. What about you? Are you alone?"

"My father is in the warehouse there inspecting a shipment of tea. He gave me permission to watch the ships, so I don't think he would object. He is doing some experiments."

His heart raced with anticipation as they walked up the gangplank. With a question or command to crewmen here and there, the captain explained the process of loading to take advantage of buoyancy and the water displacement of the ship's hull. Going below deck, if the boy had a slight concern that his father might become worried about his absence, he ignored it. He marveled at the inner workings of this wondrous self-contained vessel that would soon leave the secure and stable moorings of the port and head out over the high seas.

At one point of their tour, he was aware of increased motion of the vessel and exclaimed that the ship was moving. The captain explained, "It is only the rising due to the incoming tide. As it raises us, we will be able to cast off easily and leave the dock."

They came upon a group of about twenty people huddled close together for warmth who seemed not to be involved with the ship's operation. "Who are they?" asked the boy.

"Indentured servants. A few of them are from the prison, sent there for having committed minor offenses. Most of them are poor folk who could scarcely make a living here in England. They are going to the New World to make a better life, but they have no money for their fare. When we get to Richmond, I will sell their indentures to masters who will use their services for as many years as their contract requires. That will pay for their passage."

The boy cast a backward look at the group. What awaited them on the other side of the ocean? Would they be treated kindly? Were they virtually slaves? At least there was a time limit on their servitude, he thought.

"You've seen everything but my quarters," said the captain. "Now I'll show you what my work is here. Let's go aft."

The furnishings of the captain's quarters were much more refined than any others seen thus far. The polished desk and comfortable chairs invited further learning experiences.

"Are you acquainted with maps?" asked the captain.

"A little," said the boy, noticing the ship's log and other papers were covered up with the cartography which the captain had retrieved from the mate's room and laid out across the table.

"This will be our route," explained the captain, "Unless, of course, we are forced to make changes due to bad weather."

Minutes slipped by unheeded as the boy remained spellbound by the thrill of it all. "This is very interesting, and I do thank you for taking your valuable time to show me all this. I really must be getting back on land now, but I wish I could be going with you. Maybe one day I shall," he said at last.

He reached for the doorknob and found it unyielding. Puzzled, he turned to the captain and urgently asked to be let out. Then, looking through the porthole, he noted that outlines of other ships were passing by his view. "We *are* moving. I must leave at once," he said in alarm.

The door remained locked against his frantic efforts to open it. Filled with apprehension, he appealingly glanced at the silent, glowering captain. He began struggling with the door, shouting to be let out, until a hard blow of the captain's cane across his shoulders stopped him.

In place of the kindly, hospitable captain was a vicious, sneering tyrant. "Fas-cin-a-ted by all you've learned, are you?" he taunted. "You've a lot more to learn. I'll wager you hadn't ever felt the smart of a cane on your soft body. Well, I have, many a time. My mother's pimp used to beat me in order to get her to do what he wanted. When she saw she could no longer protect me, she told me to run away. About your age I was when I went to sea, but I didn't have your fancy clothes," he snarled.

"I worked hard for a crusty old captain; saved his hide once, too, I did," he went on boasting. "He taught me all I needed to know to be a ship's officer, and when he died he left me this ship. That's all the help I ever got and I worked for every bit of it." Those gray eyes were cold with an icy fury that made James shiver.

"Why are you doing this to me?" the boy wailed.

"Your high and mighty class has no respect for us hard-working folk. Oh, no! When my captain was alive, we'd walk by the Captain's Inn and see the owners and captains drinking and dining. He always said that they wouldn't welcome the likes of us in there. Yesterday I walked in and ordered me a tankard of ale and a meal. Well, this snooty head waiter met me and wanted to know which ship I came from. Then he said my ship was not flagged under His Majesty's Merchant Fleet, and he could not serve me since I didn't belong there. He walked me out of the door as if I was a pukin' dog." The words tumbled out in a fit of resentment over the snub.

"But I haven't done anything to you," James protested.

"You come from a family of privilege, it seems. Your gentleman father probably wouldn't give me the time of day. And yet, without any help from a wealthy family, I've become master of my own ship. That's more than you can do unless you have it handed to you on e silver platter." He was shaking his finger in the boy's face.

With mock condescension he continued, "You seem to be a sharp lad, though. Now we'll see what seven years as an indentured servant does for your respectability. That's what I'll find fascinating—my own experiment."

"You can't get by with this. My father will look for me until he finds me . . . and . . . God will punish you for this crime."

Another blow of the cane. "I don't see God here," his captor snorted. "You are in no position to threaten me. Take off your coat."

Dazed, the boy complied.

"You won't be needing this, and there'll be no fancy tailors to make you a new one where you'll be going."

"My mother made that coat," the boy protested.

"I don't want to hear about your mother," the captain raged. "Boy," shouted the captain. He handed the garment to the gangling youngster that came to the door. "Throw it overboard."

The fact that the door was left open was not lost on the boy. Jumping overboard would gain him nothing now. His eyes turned to the porthole as the ship was turned obliquely to the dock. Was his father among the figures he saw there so far away? Soon the tide would carry his coat to shore. When found, it would convince his father that he had somehow slipped in and drowned and so any further search would be abandoned.

The captain's sharp remark halted his reverie of misery. "Now then, let's get busy and make all this legal. What's your name?"

"James Bankstone."

"What are your father's connections?"

"He lectures in botany and agriculture at the university."

"I mean," the captain growled impatiently, "which are his ships and where are his land holdings?"

"We have only a small house in Oxford." James explained that the merchants of Liverpool, eager for a greater share of the tea trade of London's East India Company, had asked his father to determine why the tea in their warehouses often developed mold.

The captain was silent for a moment. He had thought the boy to be the son of one of the shipping magnates—those who tried to force out the smaller ship owners. His plan to finally deal a blow against the power structure lost some of its appeal, but it was too late to change now. "Boy," came another shout for the cabin boy, "call the purser to bring paper and pen," he ordered. "How old are you?" he asked James.

The boy answered, "Twelve."

The cane fell again. "You will say 'sir' when you answer me," the captain roared in frustration.

To the purser, who arrived fidgeting with his writing materials, he said, "Purser, what we have here is a lad who came to me just moments before we set sail. He is running away from a violent father who has made his life miserable. He's been following me about, begging me to take him on board. I've decided to have pity on him and let him sail with us to Richmond. Make out the indenture papers and state clearly the reasons why we offer him passage. When you've done that, bring them back and he will sign them, before we give him a berth with the others."

"Aye, sir," was the obedient reply as the purser departed.

James's heart sank at the realization of his plight. He would have no recourse, even if his father should pick up the trail. Legal documents would confirm the lie, the captain's defense. James's signature would eliminate the need of forgery.

He didn't know how long he waited in the room that seemed more like a prison of doom now, instead of an interesting cabin filled with exciting paraphernalia. His heart ached for his father who must be frantically searching for him. Soon he would have to return to Oxford to tell his dear wife that their son was lost.

Tears came to James's eyes at the thought of his mother. She had been his teacher as well. Eagerly he had absorbed her instructions and had pleased her by reading to her as she did housework. Then a severe bout of pneumonia had sapped her strength and left her too frail for her usual duties. James had become quite proficient in doing the household chores. In turn she read to him while she rested. She loved poetry; James preferred stories of adventure. The accounts of heroes in the Bible had led to lively discussions of justice, moral behavior, man's need for a savior, and the faithful promises of God. These were woven into the fabric of his life.

It seemed to James that there had never been a troubled moment in the home he had known. He often accompanied his father traveling the countryside, learning of the wealth of plant life in God's good earth. He had been ecstatic when his father asked him to come along on the four day coach ride to Liverpool. The bond between the three of them had been strong and yet supple enough for their individualities to flourish. Would he ever know such joy again?

Sadness and rage welled up in James. How could this man, so clever and cruel, shatter the lives of three people who had done him no wrong? His sense of the injustice gave way to a certain dignity that comes only from a clean conscience. It would stand him in good stead, no matter what people might do to him.

The purser, who doubled as second mate while at sea, had returned. "Now then, sign right here," he ordered.

James picked up the paper and began to read.

"You needn't show off that you're able to read a bit. Just sign it," the captain commanded.

James continued to read.

"You may go, Purser. I'll send it to you for your files when he has finished reading it," the captain said. The words were pleasant enough, and James saw that the purser was not to know of the criminal dealing that was going on.

He finished reading the document, dated April 10, 1742, which described him as a runaway, his father as a violent man who had abused him repeatedly, and the captain as his benefactor. It was like rubbing salt into a wound. He was being made to abet his own kidnapping and defame his father in the process. The captain's pseudo hospitality served only as a means of evaluating his vulnerability and potential value, he now realized.

"I will not sign this . . . sir," he said grimly.

"Oh yes, you will, when I get through with you," the captain threatened. The cane was used again liberally, but he soon sensed that the boy would not be intimidated by such means. "Ah, you are indeed stubborn, like me; but I can break you, and you will sign."

James had begun to fear that he might be killed, but then he realized that the captain had been trying to hide the coercion from any witnesses. A dead body would be hard to explain. The canings had occurred when only the two of them were in the room. Perhaps if he refused to sign, the captain would have to let him travel as a passenger or crewman, and he would be able to return on another ship later.

The captain was pondering his next move. Now he called, "Boy!" The tall lad must have been outside the cabin door constantly awaiting the captain's beck and call.

"Take James here down to the meat storage room below the galley. Wait for me there." The tone was not that of one who was about to become conciliatory.

As they walked, the lad asked, "Are you going to be working with the ship's cook?"

"I don't know," was the only answer. There was no use in protesting to this underling.

The storage room was dank. Cured meat hung from the rafters. In the center was a heavy table used as a cutting board. An assortment of large, sharp knives plus a whetting rod were neatly placed in a slotted rack.

James tried to believe that he would not be mutilated since he was to be sold in marketable condition. He hoped that the cook had seen them enter the room. If only he could hold out a little longer. . .

The wait for the captain was brief. He entered with his cane, carrying the paper. "It's dark and cold in here. Go get a candle and a pan of coals from the cook," he ordered. The lad disappeared and soon returned with the items.

"Would you believe, Boy, that this rascal here expects to have free passage to America and refuses to work for his fare or sign this writ of indenture? We are going to teach him that on this ship no one refuses to obey the captain. Here, tie this thong around his wrist." The captain pulled four leather thongs from his pocket.

The captain tied a thong on the opposite wrist. "Now then, on to the table, Master James." James was no match for the strength of the two, and in a moment he was lying face down on the rough cutting table with each hand tied to a table leg at one end, and his ankles tied spread-eagle at the other, his torso bare from the waist up.

"We'll loose your right hand if you will sign the paper," the captain snarled.

"It's all a lie. I'll never sign," James answered.

The blows of the cane were much more painful as they jolted his chest against the table. He clenched his teeth to keep from crying out.

"I'll not have you wasting my time. These coals will come in handy. Did you know that an indentured servant who runs away from his obligations to his master is subject to being branded so that he will be returned to his rightful owner when found? We both heard you trying to break my door down so you could run and hide. That's the same as running away." The captain had placed the whetting rod that the cook would use to sharpen his knives, into the pan of coals.

"Now remember this: My name is Captain Thomas Nash. A *T* and an *N* on your hide will leave no doubt in your mind that you belong to me. It won't be on your face; that might take away from your market value. Your back is a good enough spot for that."

The cross bar of the *T* was soon burned into the tender skin, followed by a wait to reheat the instrument before the letter was completed. "Three more for the *N*," said the captain, "unless you are ready to sign."

James quivered and moaned helplessly while the glowing rod was applied diagonally. The captain, who had vented his wrath by way of several angry outbursts, was now coldly, methodically avenging his humiliation on one of the much resented fortunate folk. He had studied to be proper in speech and attire, longing to be accepted as one of the cultured class. He promised himself that he would prove that he was a better man than any of them. This pampered youth before him would be made to accept his authority. The rod was again heating in the coals.

A knock at the door interrupted. "Captain Nash, the mate says he needs you right away on the bridge. There are two big ships at the mouth of the channel, and they are crowding us," said an excited crewman.

"I hired him on as a sailing master, and he can't even find his way out of the channel!" the captain snorted.

"Please, Captain, he says it is very urgent. I have been a long time looking for you, and he said I must find you right away."

Imperiously, the captain stalked from the room. Soon the vessel was veering, and shouts were exchanged between the officers on the bridges of the ships involved.

After a long silence, the somewhat horrified cabin boy told James, "You'd better sign. *Nobody* goes against Captain Nash."

James nodded. His right hand was loosed. Shakily, he signed his name, and then lay exhausted, dazed, and numb.

The news that the document was signed brought no appreciation from Captain Nash. "Take it to the purser, and then bring me a bottle of whiskey. I hope that idiot on the bridge can take care of things from now on."

The captain slept in a drunken stupor. The cabin boy knew he must not leave his post near the captain's quarters. Since James was obviously supposed to be put to work in the galley, the boy knew he would be released by the cook's helper.

There was no need for cured meat the next day, since the fresh meat taken on board must be used first. No one entered the storage room and the noise of activity prevented the boy's cries, and later his pleas for water, from being heard. In and out of consciousness now, James Bankstone would have welcomed death, but such relief comes not by mere will. Another day brought that event closer.

The cook's helper, sent to fetch a slab of salt pork, returned wide-eyed to his mentor. "There's a dead boy tied to the cutting table."

"What d'ya mean, a dead boy?"

"He doesn't answer and his body is cold."

The cook was a veteran seaman, inured to many of the hardships of life at sea, but the sight stirred him with pity. "Ah . . . we'll have to ask the captain what to do. Go tell him that we've found the lad. If you can't get to the captain, tell the cabin boy. They came down here together, I remember."

The question jolted Captain Nash's memory and gave him a start which he hid with difficulty. "You say he may be dead? If so, slip him overboard. If he's alive take care of him, and when he's well, put him to work." Then as the cabin boy turned to relay the message. "Explain to them that the boy was a welsher and in need of discipline."

The cook had detected the flutter of a weak pulse in James's neck. "Let's get him into the galley and see if he can swallow some of that broth."

James was wrapped in a blanket and fed in small sips until able to quench his thirst with great gulps. Slowly, he returned to consciousness and a renewed awareness of his plight. The gruff kindness of the cook and the comradeship of his helper served to ease his anguish somewhat.

There could have been no better place for him to berth during the voyage. He was a diligent worker, and there was always enough to eat. The fact that his meals were the last remains left in the big iron pots was all the better as the tiny amounts of iron wiped out with crusts of hearty black bread enriched his blood, and with that his energy and interest in life.

The long journey drew to an end at last. The port of Hampton and remains of Jamestown were by-passed, as the small ship proceeded easily with the tide up the James River. By the time the ship docked at Richmond, the cold winds and seasickness that had so plagued the passengers in steerage were forgotten. Commerce hummed along the sunny river. The banks, covered in the lavish dark green of the woods, formed a refreshing view while the ship was navigated up the tortuous course of the river.

As the passengers lined the ship's rails eagerly awaiting the moment of debarking, the sailors began uncovering the holds while others prepared the mooring ropes. The purser fidgeted with the ship's manifest, and the indentured servants were assembled near the gangplank. James had mixed feelings about leaving his two benefactors in the galley, but he hastened to take his place with the servants about to leave.

His heart and face hardened when he saw the captain approaching to inspect the human cargo. At the captain's nod, the people began leaving the ship. James stared straight ahead, hating to look at the captain, but when he came abreast of his abuser, he heard that cold, hard voice. "Well, you look to be in good enough shape. Someone who needs a growing boy for back-breaking work will be glad to have your services. Just to be sure you've learned to obey orders, kneel and kiss my boots," the captain commanded with a sneer.

Without a change of facial expression the boy complied. He knew that there would be more humiliation to bear in the years ahead, but he still cradled hope in his heart.

The captain was satisfied that he had brought the coddled youth down to the same level of despondency he himself had endured at that age. Not until he had left the ship and melted into the crowd on shore, did Captain Nash notice that a pool of spittle had been deposited on his boot in a last act of defiance.

II

Introduction to the New World

The band of ragged immigrants was silent, each wondering where his path ahead would lead. Several were quickly separated from the group. Arrangements had been made in advance for their services by the wealthy landowners who needed carpenters, metal-workers, and other skilled artisans, and were happy to pay their fare plus a small stipend for several years.

In the enclosure, prospective buyers walked among the indentured servants, questioning, inspecting for health and strength of limbs. One woman claimed to be a seamstress. She was led to the sales master, and soon a price agreement was reached. She left with her new mistress, a shopkeeper.

Those remaining who claimed no special skills were brought forward on a small stage and one by one auctioned to the highest bidder. A man and wife protested vociferously when they were about to be separated, and one bidder backed off, bringing a sharp rebuke from the auctioneer; but eventually both went to the same buyer, and the bidding continued.

A burly man in workman's clothes began bidding for the indentures of James, and with little competition the deal was soon sealed. James found himself walking at the man's side until they reached a wagon with a team of oxen hitched to it. In one giant step the man was in the seat, and with a motion of his hand indicated that James was to join him on the seat.

In silence they rode toward the outskirts of town until the man asked, "Do you know how to take care of animals?"

"No, sir, but I can learn," James replied. The answer seemed to please his new owner.

Another long silence. Then, "Don't you have any other clothes?"

"No, sir, I couldn't bring any." James was glad that he was questioned no further on that subject.

The yard they entered had a small house and one good-sized building with a loft and a solid wall only on the north, leaving the south side open. The man showed James how to unhitch the oxen, remove the yokes, and inspect for any sores caused by the pressure of pulling against a heavy load. "Give them each a forkful of hay in their trough. Then fill their water tub. Be sure to close the rail across the fence, and then come into the house."

Inside the house August Tornson looked at his wife with satisfaction. "Wilma, you are going to like him, I think. He is polite, speaks only when spoken to, and gets right to work without a word."

"I hope so. You are so goot to me, Husband. Now I can do my housevork vit someone to run and fetch vat I need, and I von't be so lonesome vile you vork such long days."

"There is one thing that we must do, and that is get him some clothes. He came with only what he wears on his back."

"You vill need to buy some clott in town den, but first I can make a shirt for him out of de good parts of de vun you tore last veek."

"Ya, that will do nice. I had the sales master read his papers. He ran away from a mean father and could bring nothing with him."

Having finished caring for the oxen, James approached the house with some trepidation and slowly opened the door. He was glad it squeaked a bit and announced his entry. How was one to knock on such a rough-hewn door?

The house was actually smaller than the stable, he thought. An all-purpose room contained a crude slab table, two stools, and an armchair in which a young woman sat. The man was dipping soup from an iron pot suspended in the fireplace into three wooden bowls and setting them on the table. The aroma from the kettle was delightful and lifted his spirits considerably.

Two pairs of eyes gazed at him silently, and he shifted nervously. "Good evening, madam," he said quietly. He was relieved to see a cheerful smile and hear the brisk voice of his mistress answer with a heavy Scandinavian accent, "Goot evening. Vat is your name?"

"James Bankstone, ma'am."

"Yames."

"James, ma'am," he repeated.

"Yames. Goot. You must be hungry. Come and eat." A stern look from his master told James that his name would be "Yames" where his mistress was concerned, and that she was not to be corrected. So, he was to eat with them. This arrangement alone served to allay his apprehension as to what servitude would be like. He noted that his mistress had not risen to come to the table but remained sitting in her chair. He watched as the man slid her chair to the table on the runners that had been added. She was an invalid. He began to see what his role would be in the household.

The soup was hearty and good. A sense of well-being began to evolve among the three diners. With his bowl nearly empty, James suddenly thought of meals he had eaten with his parents. Sadness deepened the lines around his mouth and forehead. Momentarily he fought back tears, but not so successfully that he was not seen by his mistress. He was grateful that she looked at him intently only for an instant and then addressed a question to her husband which required all that man's attention. What would he have thought if he had seen a twelve-year old boy crying? Emotional displays seemed totally out of character for such a gruff giant of a man.

It seemed quite natural to James to pick up the bowls without being told after supper, but he stopped, puzzled as to where they were to be washed. Mrs. Tornson read his mind and said, "At de bench outside; dere is soap and enough vater in de pail." Getting water for the household as well as for the animals would be a big part of his chores, he thought.

Before falling asleep on his straw pallet that night, he heard his new owners talking in Swedish in their tiny bedroom. Once or twice he thought he heard his name mentioned. He couldn't know that the man teased his wife with, "I thought you said he'd have to sleep in the hay loft because you would not have a young scoundrel sleeping in the house." She retorted with, "He is not a scoundrel; he is a good boy." The man smiled in the darkness. Life would be better now. His energetic wife would again be able to work at her tasks after a disappointing healing of a broken hip. The boy would be a help to both of them, and they would be giving him a good home. Soon August Tornson was snoring.

The darkness had lifted only a little when James became aware of heavy footsteps near his head. Before he could sit upright, his master was already out the door to begin the day's work. Quickly James folded his pallet and went to the stable. He heard the man talking in lively and authoritative tones, but soon realized he was talking in Swedish to his oxen. Upon seeing the boy at his side, the master was glad he had used his native tongue. The boy didn't need to know the pet names and the morning pep talks he gave his beloved animals.

"I must leave early. People who had shipments come in yesterday will want a drayman to haul it to their homes. I want to be the first one at the docks. Today you must clean all the dirty straw out of these stalls and put in fresh. Fetch plenty of water to fill the barrels. Then help my wife when she needs you."

"Yes, sir. I'll do my best."

Copying the deft movements his master used to hitch one ox to the wagon, James managed the same for the other one. Then he was left holding the reins as Mr. Tornson went back into the house to lift his wife into her chair and bring her into the main room. Without a further word he drove away.

In the house a flurry of activity began. Ashes needed to be cleared out of the fireplace. A goodly supply of firewood was brought in and would soon be half used up as Mrs. Tornson began delightedly to bake bread and pastries. Several hens' nests were robbed of the eggs which had accumulated over the past two days, so that she could make the filling for the pastries.

The activity loosened her tongue, and she was soon supplying answers to James's unasked questions. "It feels goot to cook again. Ven I fell and broke my hip two monts ago, I couldn't do nudding. Now anyhow I can stand here vid my cane and use de dings you bring to me. . . . My family is all in de old country. I came alone last year ven August sent de money to come marry him." The account went on.

It was dark when Mr. Tornson returned. The oxen were tired, as were all the people of the household. James hurried to unhitch the oxen. "They've had a long hard day. Be good to them." Already James was comfortable with that task.

The next morning James was surprised to find that he had awakened before the others. He thought his master would be pleased if he hitched the oxen and had them ready to go. When no one came to drive the wagon, puzzled, he returned to the house.

In a half hour Mr. Tornson came out of the bedroom yawning. "Sunday. Today we all rest," he said. Shamefaced, James realized that in eight weeks at sea, with every day like the next, he had lost track of time. As he rose to loose the oxen, Mr. Tornson strode to the door, stretching his arms and shoulders, and spotted the waiting team. "Let them graze in the woods behind the stable, but first tie the bell on one of them. We must find them and bring them back before sunset."

Sunday morning breakfast was special—eggs, ham, fresh bread, and apple butter. When James could hold it in no longer, he asked, "Are we going to church this morning?"

An uncomfortable silence ended with the statement, "We are Lutherans from the old country." Eager, the boy wanted to offer to read from the scriptures, but then realized that there were no books in sight, nor, for that matter was there any paper, except for the one that the terms of his indenture were written on. He kept silent, wondering if either of these two could read, even in their own language. He experienced a new feeling of deprivation. Would he ever read or study again? Thoughts of a home far away filled him with sadness.

The hours passed slowly, and then awkwardly. For the Tornsons it was strange to have an outsider present during their leisure time. James didn't know if he was to remain at their beck and call, or vanish from their presence. Then an idea came to him. "If you don't need me to do anything for a while, may I go to the stream and wash my clothes?" he asked.

There was instant relief of the situation. "Yes, of course," said Mr. Tornson. "There is no work to be done until evening."

The water felt wonderful on his body. The clothes so badly in need of washing had been pounded, rubbed, rinsed, and now lay drying on the grass. Things could be much worse, he reasoned, as he lay on his back in the June sunshine and watched the clouds, and the birds circling overhead. He almost pitied Captain Nash and his poisonous resentment until he thought of his parents. Had they resigned themselves to losing him? Did they really believe him to be dead?

The sun was not yet low in the sky when he returned to the house. Mrs. Tornson looked up eagerly as he entered. "I made dis for you; try it on," she said holding up a shirt. "For pants I need more clott, but my man brought it yesterday. It vill soon be ready."

It fit perfectly for a work shirt, with roomy shoulders and sleeves. "Thank you very much," he said.

"My wicked wife worked on a Sunday to finish it. I fear for her," Mr. Tornson said with a mirthful twinkle in his eye.

"Oh, hush!" she retorted. "You know vat de Bible says about de ox in de vell."

"For me, the well was the stream . . . and I *did* smell like an ox," James joined in.

A chorus of laughter filled the little house. Mrs. Tornson clapped her hands and exclaimed gleefully, "He knows his Bible."

In the uneasy silence that followed, James looked at them and with a slight quiver in his voice, the words burst forth, "Thank you. Thank you both for your kindness."

They were both smiling benignly at him until the man cleared his throat and said, "Just don't disappoint us. Don't get lazy, tell lies, or steal. We will get along all right."

A little taken aback, but realizing that his master was not given to sentiment, James responded, "Yes, sir. I will go find the oxen now," and with that he walked to the woods.

"Oh, August, vy must you be so stern? He has had so little love in his life and he tries so hard to please us. How could his fadder be so mean to beat him vittout mercy? Yesterday ven he finished cleaning de stable, his sweaty shirt clung to his back and I could see velts from de beatings. I vanted so much to hug him."

"Go slow, woman. He has been here less than a week. By the time he has been here seven years, we will know him better, and I hope, love him even more."

"You could take him into your business den. It vould be like a fadder and son."

He did not contradict her. "Well, we wait and see."

There was no time for laziness. Mrs. Tornson, with new-found energy, was determined to make up for time lost due to her injury. She was a meticulous housekeeper, which meant that James had many jobs to do. There was more to women's work than he realized. Every Monday clothes were to be washed and bedding aired. The floor, as well as the table, were scrubbed frequently.

Outside there was hay to be unloaded when his master returned. Walking in the woods to retrieve the oxen, he discovered plants he had never seen before. Sometimes he brought bouquets of wild flowers which his mistress received with pleasure. He vowed that one day he would dig some up and plant them near the house so she could enjoy them.

Weeks turned into months, and the days became shorter, the sun less intense. The master's drayage business kept him very busy. He seemed pleased with the income he brought home.

One day he proudly brought in a shiny new axe. "This is much better than the old one." To James he said, "Two or three trees near the edge of the yard need to be cut down. We must build a fence to make the pen bigger. I will buy a cow and next spring there will be a calf. We will plant a garden in the open space. My woman will like that. Get used to swinging the axe. On my next free day we will start cutting."

September was as busy as the months before it. Not as interested in ships as he had once been, James was still curious about the varied cargo his master hauled. As he cleaned out the wagon each evening, he tried guessing what merchandise had filled it that day.

One day he found something that set his heart to racing and his mind whirring. There, hidden under a torn piece of burlap was an almost whole sheet of paper with nothing written on it. He smoothed it out carefully. How could he send a message to his parents so far away? What could he use to write with? "Supper" came the call from the house. He reached up to tuck the precious paper under the hay in the loft.

Evenings were pleasant with the couple, but James felt lonesome, restless, and homesick. He had tried picking up a few words of their conversation, but mostly it remained an incomprehensible dialogue. Bringing in a large block of wood to center amid the coals, he banked the embers and hot ashes around it to keep a spark of fire until morning. A piece of cold wood charcoal caught his eye. Would this be good for making ink?

The thought made him nearly dizzy with excitement. He usually sat outside in the evening breeze after work with his memories and fantasies of his future. This evening he looked for two smooth rocks before the twilight turned to darkness. Now by the light from the open door he crushed the charcoal into a fine powder. What was next? What could be the binding agent? It would need to be fluid and yet not too easily absorbed by the paper. Would it fade? One experiment after another seemed to lead him closer to his goal . . . a tiny bit of grease from the wagon wheel, some scrapings of rust, maybe a bit of oil or water to thin it. It was time to lay it aside now as he noted that the candle inside had burned nearly down, a sure sign of bedtime.

He lay on his pallet, composing a letter to his parents. He must be brief, using words that would allay their concern. Would his father come and get him? He would have to give his master's name in order to be found. Could the postal system be trusted in these colonies? Surely there had to be a system for communicating with England. This was England's most prized colony, after all, named for the revered Virgin Queen.

The next morning dawned with a steady rain falling and a touch of autumn in the air. His experimental ink was drenched. He could make more. The drayman still had promises to keep to his customers. He would go into town and wait for a break in the weather, or else find a way of protecting the loads from the rain.

"Dis is a goot day to start spinning de vool," Mrs. Tornson said. "Ven I could not do my housevork, I could still spin, and I have made a goot start, but ven de veatter was so hot, I put it avay. Now it is time to make some vinter clotting. My man vill need a sveater. He vorks in all kinds of veatter."

Following her instructions, James set up the spinning wheel, brought the sack of wool, and soon was involved in the process, adjusting the spindle and rolling the yarn. Another skill learned, he thought; even though I haven't read, written, or ciphered anything for months.

The activity continued without much mental concentration required, and this proved to be the ideal situation for chatter. James listened enthralled as she told stories of her childhood in Sweden; how she and August had shyly watched each other from a distance; her sorrow when she heard that he was leaving their home town to work on a ship. She had thought that one day he would ask her to be his wife; instead, he was leaving. Her parents said he was a wild, irresponsible boy who would never settle down. In her heart she had yearned for him, but told her parents nothing of it. Then one day a letter came. He was in Pennsylvania working in a German settlement. They were good farmers, and it was a good country.

In the spring came another letter. The winter had been very hard with many successive days of extreme cold. He had heard that it was warmer further south, more like the winters in the south of Sweden. He was going there and would write again. The next time he would be sending money for her to come and join him; so he hoped that she would begin persuading her parents to give permission for her to marry him. "Dat August—always so sure of himself, so ready to try a new adventure."

That image of his master was intriguing. James smiled inwardly, remembering his first impression of a dull plodder. Still, there was a certain grim, no-nonsense air about him that served notice that he was not to be crossed, and that he would resent being found inadequate in any situation.

Could he tell her his story, he wondered? Would she believe it? Even if she did, would she persuade her husband to believe it also? He realized that to them he still appeared to be a runaway from an abusive home. Perhaps this kind woman felt that questioning him would only recall sad memories.

The rain continued on and off most of the day. Mr. Tornson returned wet and tired to find a cheerful fire in the hearth and a pot of savory meat and potatoes steaming. What a cure for weariness! James hastened to untie the wet boots and take the wet jacket to hang near the fireplace. "Bring him the pair of heavy socks ve vashed Monday and a dry shirt," clucked Mrs. Tornson.

James ran to the stable to take care of the oxen. They deserved extra rubbing and brushing this evening, too, along with the quiet, calming talk he had heard his master use when he thought no one was in earshot.

As he turned to leave, James heard a faint mewing sound and looked up to see bright eyes gazing down at him from the loft. "Well, what are you doing here, pretty kitty?" he asked. The animal seemed reassured and allowed itself to be approached. Slowly he reached toward it and after a moment's hesitation it reached out a paw to him. Gently, he lifted it toward him. How would the Tornsons feel about having a cat brought into the house? There was only one way to find out. "Look what I found in the loft," he announced.

Mrs. Tornson reacted warmly. "So beautiful a cat! And she is vet and lost. Her paws are sore from valking many a mile."

"At least she didn't have to work in the rain," Mr. Tornson grumbled.

"Oh, Husband, ve have baked a peach pastry for you. Here, it vill make you feel dat de day vas not all vasted."

"Woman, you are trying to shame me," he answered with imitation testiness, "but I still will not share my bed and table with a stray cat."

Eagerly James said, "I will gladly let her sleep with me near the hearth. She may only need some food and a place to rest before she travels on."

"Ya. On the other hand, you and my wife will spoil her so that she will never leave," he muttered, but he did not forbid it.

James and his mistress exchanged conspiratorial smiles and soon the cat was eagerly devouring food both of them conveniently left on their plates.

When James returned from cleaning the dishes, he saw the cat on Mrs. Tornson's lap and reasoned that the only way she could have gotten there was by way of his master's big gentle hands. "I name her 'Hilda,'" his mistress said, adding, "The only Svedish cat in Virginia." At bedtime, however, the cat became his companion.

There were more rainy days now. Most roads had become quagmires. "Winter will soon be here, and not many ships will come in, but now everyone is in a hurry to have their goods delivered. If only the rain would stay away a few more weeks," the drayman fussed.

When it began clearing, the man and boy took the axes to the trees. James was no match for the man, but he tried valiantly, and soon sore muscles became a daily problem. With Hilda's furry body snuggled against his shoulders, the pain would ease enough to permit sleep at night.

Impatiently, the man decided to try to make deliveries if he could find passable roads after a few day of sunshine. When he had not returned by noon, his wife knew he was putting in a long day at his work. "It looks like de man's rest days are over," she commented.

"Rest! They didn't feel like rest to me," James exclaimed. Instantly, he wondered if it sounded like a complaint.

"Your shoulders are very sore, I know. Look, let me rub dem vit dis fat and pepper mixture. It vill make dem feel varm and not so stiff. Take off your shirt," Mrs. Tornson said.

It was natural to comply with her command, but too late he remembered that his back no longer looked like that of other twelve-year old boys. After a shocked gasp, she rubbed the shoulder and back muscles, and he could feel his muscles relaxing.

She could keep quiet no longer. "De man vas an animal to beat and burn you like dis. It's no vonder you ran avay from such a terrible fadder."

James leaped to his feet, shouting, "No, no, no. It was *not* my father; he never beat me. It was the ship's captain who kidnapped me and made out the indentures who did this to me," and suddenly he began to cry. Pent-up emotions so long restrained were released as turbulent sobbing shook his frame.

Startled, his mistress said nothing until the outburst had subsided into quiet weeping. "Do you vant to talk about it?", she asked. He nodded. The story was quickly told without relating the hours of fear, despair, and agony between the chief events.

For a long while she said nothing, and then in a voice that was not unkind she stated, "Maybe ve should get to vork now."

Emotionally spent, James performed his tasks mechanically. Slowly it dawned on him that if he were to attempt writing to his parents, it should be done now. Charcoal was again ground into a fine powder. The blend of experimental ingredients seemed to be more suitable this time. He found a chicken feather in the stable, sharpened it to a tip, spread out that hoarded sheet of paper and wrote: Dear Parents, I hope you are well. I was kidnapped and am now in Richmond, Virginia, serving Mr. and Mrs. August Tornson. Your son, James.

The ink dried slowly, but at day's end had not smudged. He folded the paper and prayed for the right moment and the right words for requesting his master to mail it. Now, as he wrote the address on the outside, his hand trembled and several blots were added. He slept that night only because his excitement succumbed to his exhaustion.

He was awake earlier than usual and had the oxen hitched. He had heard the Tornsons talking late into the night and knew that she had related his story. He had experienced too much in the past six months not to feel some apprehension when facing his master this morning.

The moment arrived and it seemed to him that Mr. Tornson was avoiding him. No look, no greeting was forthcoming. The man swung into the wagon seat and picked up the reins. "Please, sir," James began, trying to sound confident, "I found this paper in the trash you asked me to clean out of the wagon. I made some ink out of charcoal, and now I've written a letter to my parents. Would you please post it in town?"

Now at last his master looked at him, but still said nothing. James hastened to add, "I understand that there will be a charge for the postage, but I will work harder than ever."

When there was still no answer, he added, "You'll see; I'll have that tree chopped down just as soon as I can."

The man tucked the letter into his pocket but still gave no answer. The oxen were given the signal to go, and the wagon moved out to the road, leaving the boy wondering. He remembered the times his master did not commit himself, but simply did not refuse before complying. He felt fairly certain that his letter would be mailed.

The axe was used mightily that day. Mrs. Tornson said not a word about their conversation and seemed unwilling to discuss what James most wanted to know: Had his master believed him?

III

Of No Reputation

Hilda showed no inclination to leave. As her paws healed she began walking about the room more, often rubbing herself against Mrs. Tornson's legs. "So, vere did you come from, pretty Hilda? You are yentle and polite. Somebody treated you vit love, but who?" the mistress murmured. James was glad that Hilda would be keeping her company. He would be busy with the axe trying to compensate his master for the price of postage for that precious letter.

Autumn rains were an almost daily occurrence as October drew to a close. The transplants James had taken from the woods grew lush and sturdy, developing a good root system to carry them through the winter. All the wool had been spun into yarn and was rolled into neat balls ready for use. "Go to the shelf in the bedroom and bring me my knitting needles," was Mrs. Tornson's request as she settled herself to the task of sweater making, satisfied that her fall house cleaning was properly done.

"The stream is out of its banks today and may still rise," said Mr. Tornson one morning.

"Surely it vill not reach de house?" she asked.

"No, I don't believe so. But things like rats and snakes will leave their holes in the banks and come to higher ground."

"Hilda will have a job to keep the rats and mice away," James surmised.

"Maybe not. She is going to have babies in one or two weeks," Mr. Tornson replied.

"Are you sure?" his wife asked.

"Oh yes," he answered. "A man who takes care of animals knows such things."

"Ya. My husband from de farm knows about how life goes on. My fadder vas a fisherman. I learned notting from de fish."

"But my mouth waters for the taste of one of your mother's good cod dinners."

"Shh, don't make me homesick."

They fell silent. Hilda seemed to want to brighten the mood and rubbed against Mr. Tornson's legs. He reached down to pick her up and held her in his lap, stroking her thoughtfully. Mrs. Tornson and James smiled at each other.

"Maybe I could catch some fish in the stream," James volunteered.

"Some time when there is nothing else to do," said the master. "I want very much to get that other tree down and start splitting it into fence rails. Then we must clear the weeds away from where the trees stood so that we can till it in the spring. Wilma, by this time next year you will have reaped a good harvest of vegetables for the winter. Now I must take all the drayage jobs I can get in order to buy our food. Next year I may be hauling some of our own produce to market." They nodded contentedly.

At the next sunny day the drayman left at noon to find work. The stream had not totally receded, but the ground was drying out nicely near the house.

"Do me a favor before you go," Mrs. Tornson requested. "Take my shair outside and help me down de step, so dat I can sit in de sun dis afternoon. I have not been outside for so long, and vinter vill soon be here."

Affectionately, he did so. "Now you must promise me that you will not try to walk on this rough ground," Mr. Tornson said. She nodded agreement. "And James, you must check on her often." James understood that to mean that he was to work on the tree in between checking on her welfare. "I will be back early. Be careful."

The knitting needles continued to fly but with long pauses between spurts, as the mistress gazed at what was to be her garden area in the spring. If they enriched the soil with refuse from the stables, starting now, she would be able to plant many things close together. She might even try some corn which Americans seemed to like so much, but mostly potatoes, beans, cabbage, carrots, and greens. Surely those would grow as well as they did in Sweden.

"Would you like some water to drink?" asked James, startling her out of her day-dreaming. He looked much in need of some, too, as he held a cup in one hand and wiped his brow with the other.

"No, tank you, maybe later. You drink . . . and rest a vile."

"Drink I must; resting I can do later," he said and returned to chopping.

The ball of yarn had dropped to the ground and rested on the edge of the blanket, but Hilda made no move to play with it as she was wont to do. She slept more these days, and her abdomen grew larger.

As James approached his mistress the second time, he was surprised to see Hilda on her feet, standing rigidly, eyes fixed on an object on the ground at the side of the chair. Coming closer, he heard what he thought was the sound of a locust or similar beetle making its rasping sounds. Horrified, he saw the snake, light brown with diamond-shaped markings on its back, efficiently camouflaged amid the fallen leaves, but now aroused. Its tail, tipped with rattles, vibrated furiously. It had spotted the ball of yarn moving as it was pulled toward the needles. It had smelled the animal, and it was hungry, but now it was also frustrated and dangerous.

"Madam, don't move." The words were so urgent they sounded sharp. "Don't pull any yarn up or move at all."

Now Mrs. Tornson's eyes followed his gaze and she saw the snake. "Hilda, come here," she wailed. It would have been a mistake, but fortunately, Hilda continued to mesmerize the snake with her stare.

James knew he needed to draw the snake away. He ran back for the axe and picked up a long stick. Coming closer, he rapped sharply on the ground, and the snake darted its head his way. Immediately Hilda jumped on it, sinking her sharp teeth into the back of its neck. She was not able to hold down the reptile, but she held on to its neck as the snake coiled, rolled, and thrashed about, tossing her back and forth and slamming her body into the ground.

None too soon the boy was able to pin it down with the stick and with the axe sever the head from the lower section, which continued to coil, recoil, and rattle for some minutes. Only then did Hilda release her hold. Breathing hard, she returned to her position at her mistress's feet.

"God be praised," exclaimed Mrs. Tornson.

"Amen," James echoed, as they shared a moment of gratitude.

Picking up Hilda, she said, "You bote deserve a revard. You have saved my life."

In a few hours Mr. Tornson returned, noting that the clear skies meant an early evening chill, and eager to bring his wife into the security of the house. What he heard was enough to make him hold her especially close as he carried her in. To James he spoke a heartfelt, "Thank you." All hearts were merry as they gathered to prepare and eat the evening meal.

Mrs. Tornson seemed stimulated by the excitement. She talked and knitted rapidly by candle light and then called for another candle to be lit, saying that she was not yet sleepy.

Mr. Tornson went outside to inspect the snake and marveled that Hilda had been able to hold on for even a moment, for it was a full-grown specimen with six rattles. "They say," he commented, "that these snakes add a rattle each year. But they are not often found this far north."

Hilda seemingly had lost all interest in what had been her prey. She gave the reptile a wide berth as she watched Mr. Tornson cut off the rattles and bring them in the house. "Vy do you bring such a horrible ding into de house?" Mrs. Tornson protested as he placed them on the mantel.

He answered, "To remind us to be watchful; also, to be thankful."

When at last their conversation ended, they looked over at James and saw him fast asleep. "Such a goot boy," she said.

"So far," Mr. Tornson replied.

The next day dawned clear and cool. "Ve must vash clottes today before more rain comes, since ve have missed so many good vash days," Mrs. Tornson asserted.

James knew the routine: fetch water to fill the pot over a fire in the yard. When near boiling, remove half of it to another pot to which cold water is added. Cut soap from the bar into the boiling water and add the linen, and later, the heavy cotton clothes. When they are boiled use the same water for the heavy work clothes. Everything would be rinsed with clear water. Today that would be easy since the supply would come from the rain water that had been caught cascading from the roof. He could do it all properly without his mistress's supervision; so she kept busy with her knitting.

"I'll have dis finished yust in time for de cold veater,' Mrs. Tornson said with satisfaction. "Hilda seems restless today. Do you tink she is still expecting a snake?"

"Maybe, but the stream is within its banks again, and the snakes and their food—the mice and rats—can go back to their homes."

When James went to the stables the next morning it was still dark, but Hilda had been prowling about his head; so it must be time to rise. It was also uncomfortably cold. In a little while he returned to the house. "It's so cold, I'll wear two shirts this morning," he said, grabbing the garment from the peg in the wall.

As he started out the door, he found it blocked by his master who was wearing a grim expression. "Where is it?" he demanded.

"What?" asked the boy, puzzled.

"You know. The sweater my wife finished last night and left on the chair."

"I don't know. It was there the last time I saw it."

"But where is it now?" Mr. Tornson's words had a hard edge.

"I don't know. Honest!"

"Look, there are only three people in this house. I didn't take it; my wife didn't take it; so where have you put it?"

"I didn't take it either. What would I do with your sweater?"

"You may have planned to sneak away and sell it . . . maybe to buy the paper and ink you want so you can write your fanciful letters."

Sensing an ugly situation developing, James said nothing, his thoughts spinning, trying to make some sense of it.

"The sweater was on the chair last night. Neither I nor my wife left the house. You are the only one to go out this door. I am going out to hitch the oxen myself, and when I come back, that sweater had better be back on that chair," Mr. Tornson stated.

"But I don't know where it is, how . . . ?"

"Then you had better start looking," the master interrupted, and stalked out.

James could think of no explanation for the disappearance of the sweater. He glanced at Mrs. Tornson who was pale, sad, and silent. In panic, he began searching the corners of the room, removing the cushions of her chair, folding up his pallet. "May I search in your bedroom?" he asked.

Shakily, she grabbed his sleeve. "Yames, de sveater vas for *you.* I let you tink it vas for August because I vanted to surprise you. Tell him vere you put it, and it vill be all right. I hurried to finish it last night so you could have it as kind of a revard for killing de snake."

He looked at her with astonishment, disappointment, and indignation. Both of these people he had come to love thought him to be a thief. Summoning what composure he could muster, he replied, "Madam, I did not take the sweater. I do not know where it is, but thank you for thinking I deserve a reward."

"So," came a loud voice from the door, "you give yourself a reward for doing what any man would do to save another. Now you also take from my wife the pleasure of giving you the gift. I see you have not returned the sweater, but believe me, you will tell me where you have put it. Up against the wall, you scoundrel."

The color drained from James's face as he saw the ox whip in his master's hand. He had never seen it used on the oxen but supposed that it was employed for extra encouragement when they needed to put forth extra effort to overcome an obstacle. Slowly, he turned his face to the wall bracing himself with the palms of his hands.

The lash was followed by a bellow, "I mean it. Tell us."

James said nothing and the lash fell again. This could not be happening, but the pain was very real. Was there nothing he could say to stop it? His frustration boiled over as the flogging continued. He whirled to face his master. "How can I tell you when I don't know? Even if you beat me to death, I can't tell you anything," he screamed.

"August, stop! No more. Please, stop," Mrs. Tornson sobbed. The whip clattered to the floor. The man put his arm around his wife's shoulders as they turned away from the boy.

The pain of being scorned aggravated the pain of the stripes. James stood numbed by the rapid change of events.

"Get ready to go into town. I am taking you to the auction. There was a ship in the mouth of the river yesterday, so there will be others sold today. I will not have a thief and a liar in my house one more night," Mr. Tornson ordered.

James removed the shirt his mistress had made, folded it with the pants, laid them on the table, and stood silently at the door, nothing in his hands. "The clothes are yours," Mrs. Tornson said.

"My mother made these clothes. I'll not take any of yours," was the barely audible reply.

"But your muscles are about to pop out of your sleeves," she remonstrated.

"Take them," bellowed the master. "I'll not take a half-naked waif to town. Put them on."

James complied, saying in a voice that did not quite control a quiver, "I have always obeyed you; so I do now." He got into the wagon, seating himself on the floor. In a moment they were on the way to the city.

A heavy silence hung between them. Perhaps the man asked himself if he could possibly be mistaken; but then his logic told him that no one else could have committed the theft. They should never have trusted a runaway.

For his part, James tried to think of nothing, but the mind does not let go so easily. He remembered the captain's words, "You never felt a beating. I did many times." Is this what it was like to be without friends, without influence, or even reputation? A vision of his parents flashed before him, and he remembered a question he had wanted to ask but had feared to do so. What difference could it make now since he was discredited with his master anyway?

"Sir," he said, trying to be calm, "I need to know if you mailed my letter."

For a while he thought he would not get an answer. Then Mr. Tornson cleared his throat and said, "The postal agent would accept only mail going to other colonies."

"But there must be another postal system that takes mail to Europe. Your wife told me that you sent letters to Sweden."

"That was in Pennsylvania. Things were different there."

"Then you didn't mail my letter! Where is it?" James persisted.

"You had my name in it. I don't want anything to do with your lies," Mr. Tornson sniffed.

"But that was only so that my father would know where to find me if he came. Where is the letter?" the boy demanded.

Petulantly the man reached into his coat pocket and threw a crumpled paper onto the floor of the wagon. It had been soaked by repeated rains and came apart in his hands as James tried to unfold it. He was too overcome to say anything more. He would remember August Tornson—so sure of himself, not literate in English, and too proud to admit it to his servant. They would soon part company.

IV

A New Trade

The auction building seemed less formidable this time. Perhaps James was developing a measure of immunity to the hard knocks that had become such a part of his life since last spring. He looked at the people about him. Were they the victims of the inhumanity of others? Why were some called upon to suffer unjustly? He felt a measure of dignity and peace return, reminding himself that he was innocent of crimes and his conscience was clear. God was still alive and would deliver him one day as he had Joseph of the Bible.

The new arrivals of indentured servants from the ship began filing into the enclosure, and contract buyers sized up their prospective purchases. "Can you read and write?' asked a short, balding, nervous man.

"Yes, sir," James answered.

"Come with me," the man ordered and James was soon walking with his new master along streets and around corners, ending at a building with a sign that read "Gilmore Print Shop." James was about to learn the printing trade.

As they entered the warm workroom, James thought, "I won't be needing a sweater here." He was to learn that the room was kept warm to keep the ink at a constant viscosity. He remembered that Mr. Gilmore had felt of his muscles before asking if he could read. Now he understood that operating the clumsy press would keep his muscles active. He quickly learned to don an apron to protect his clothing from the ink that seemed to find its way everywhere. He was careful not to smudge the paper being printed for their clients. He smiled at the irony of his recent struggle to make ink.

From having nothing to read at the Tornsons, he was now spending most of his time reading, re-reading, arranging type, and inking the letters. It was interesting work for the most part.

Christmas and the new year were close at hand. The print shop had orders for calendars and advertisements for the shops, plus a weekly newspaper to print. They even received an important order from Williamsburg when the press there was temporarily out of order. It was a greeting from King George II to His Excellency Governor Gooch, brought by the governor's messenger, to be reprinted for distribution to all government officials in the colony. Mr. Gilmore wore himself to a frazzle getting it precisely right, fussing over each sheet that came off the press.

At last Christmas came and went. James had hardly enough time to take care of his clothes and get a breath of fresh air in the evening. He was not to be a part of the Gilmore household. He met Mrs. Gilmore only when she brought the meals, which were eaten at a side table in the workroom. He slept on a pile of sacks at the back of the workroom after he had cleaned the premises of the day's litter.

The day after Christmas, traditionally observed by the servants of the household, brought a small bit of cheer—a serving of plum pudding and two pieces of material with the explanation that Mrs. Gilmore would arrange to have clothes made from them when she found time to do so. The gift was delivered by the other worker, the master's nephew, who then returned to the circle of family. James told himself that he would not be hurt by these who showed so little warmth and concern for his well-being.

It was now that James composed a second letter to his parents, written on a piece of scrap paper. Getting it mailed would be another matter, but he folded it carefully and put it at the bottom of the small box of personal articles he kept under the sacks. Without friends or family, the holidays seemed especially drear; but these too would come to an end, he consoled himself.

The city of Richmond and all of Virginia were growing rapidly with the expansion of the tobacco industry and the influx of Negro slaves to work the plantations of wealthy landowners, some of whom had royal land grants.

Since the expedition of former Governor Alexander Spottswood across the Blue Ridge Mountains into the Shenandoah Valley, settlers had been moving westward in great numbers, many arriving from the Old World and some even from other colonies. There followed stories of conflict with the Indians and the French in the land across the mountains. Every newspaper printed was eagerly purchased and read. The editor brought in so much news each week that a second page was added, and soon after that the Richmond Gazette became a four-page weekly. It was the joy of James's life to keep up with all the happenings, to be a part of this exciting time.

Winter gave way to spring, but this year there were no walks in the woods for the young man. One day he thought of the bushes he had transplanted at the Tornson house and wondered if they would bloom this season. Resolutely he put an end to thoughts of them, but his experiences with them had not yet ended.

"The gentleman at the counter wants to speak with you," Mr. Gilmore told him one morning. Wiping his hands, he approached to face August Tornson.

"James, I came to show you something," he said, placing a package wrapped in burlap on the counter. He unrolled it, and there was the sweater. "I was clearing the last of the old hay out of the loft and found it in the farthest corner."

James stiffened. "I did not put it there," he said evenly.

"I know," was the reply, as the man unfolded the sweater to reveal a tangle of dried skin and the delicate skeletal bones of infant animals. "We think Hilda had her babies early that morning because of her fight with the snake. They were born dead; and so she never brought them down to the house. She must have dragged the sweater up the ramp to the loft when you went out the door the first time that morning."

It was James who finally broke the silence. "I'm glad that you found it. I know how much it meant to you."

There was more emotion in Mr. Tornson's face and voice than James had ever seen. "We are very sorry," were the only words he uttered.

"So was I," James blurted. He told himself that he really couldn't help delivering that bit of sarcasm.

Just then Mr. Gilmore called, "Hurry, boy. You are needed here."

"Excuse me," James said, and turned to go back to work. In a backward glance he saw his former master move through the doorway brushing a hand across his eyes. The sweater still lay on the counter. Nothing had been said about his keeping it. Impulsively, he snatched it up and ran out the door after the man. "Sir, you left the sweater," James said, placing the bundle in his hands.

That only added to the anguish in Mr. Tornson's face. They stood looking at each other intently. Then James spoke. "Thank you for coming. You could have not told me."

"No, I couldn't keep it quiet. We have had no peace since you left. James, please try to forgive us." It was almost a whisper.

"Of course," James said and extended his hand which was grasped by both of the man's big ones. "Wilma wants very much to see you. Would you come and visit us?"

"I don't get much time off here . . . none actually . . . but maybe at Easter time Mr. Gilmore will let me come." He could hear the irate voice of his master shouting for him. "I must go back. He'll be very annoyed."

That was an understatement. James ran into the shop to face a livid taskmaster. "What do you mean running out into the street and leaving ink drying on the press?" James tried to slip past him to work the press; but the temperamental Mr. Gilmore was more intent on venting his anger just then. He raised his cane even as he grabbed James by one arm. But the cane never landed.

A big strong hand held the end of the upraised instrument and Mr. Gilmore turned to face Mr. Tornson as James twisted free and ran to the press. A quick check, and he brought the ink and paper together for just the right length of time. It was a better copy than those his master had fussed over and rushed impatiently.

James could hear the men around the corner from the workroom. Tornson's voice was forceful, insistent. "You will not beat him for this. I am his former master, and I know he does his best always. He left only for a moment and that to help me. Now, I would like to buy back his contract and take him home."

Mr. Gilmore, accustomed to ingratiating himself to customers and anyone who would assert himself at the counter, became a placating negotiator. "You are coming with this proposition at a very bad time for me. You see, I've spent many hours training this boy, and now that he knows the work—and I have *much* work—I can hardly replace him."

"I will pay the full price of the original indentures. That's five pounds more than you paid for them."

"But my business would suffer more loss than that."

At this point, Mr. Tornson's voice carried into the workroom. "James, do you want to come with me?"

James could only answer, "I have nothing to say about it."

It was not the answer Mr. Tornson had hoped for, although he knew it to be true. In a lower voice now Mr. Gilmore was heard to say, ". . . not at any price you could afford." That ended the conversation. Apparently Mr. Gilmore had determined that the drayman was not important enough to warrant satisfying his request.

Comforting thoughts entered James's mind. That evening he sat on the back steps of the print shop enjoying the balmy spring breeze, looking up into a star-studded sky, recalling snatches of conversation he had overheard: ". . . five pounds more than you paid." August Tornson was not one to part with his money easily, and yet he offered that much more to be able to take him back. ". . . not at any price you could afford." Mr. Gilmore had never complimented him, and yet he would not release him for a profit. "It's good to know that I'm not worthless," he mused.

It was a year now since he had walked onto that ship. He had survived mistreatment, injustice, and back-breaking labor, and still had his self-respect despite the predictions to the contrary by Captain Nash. It felt good to forgive the Tornsons. Everybody makes mistakes sometimes. He reckoned his own grievous offense was to his parents. His father had allowed him to watch the ships from the front of the warehouse. Instead, he had crossed over the road to the docks. If he had obeyed, the captain would not have been able to carry out his scheme. What anguish his parents must have suffered when he disappeared without a trace! The letter! That must be mailed soon, and now he knew what else he must do.

The opportunity came the next evening. It was Saturday. The shop was closed down. Mr. Gilmore was about to leave broad hints of what James should do on Sunday behind closed doors, for he would not allow his servant to be idle, but didn't want his labor on the Lord's Day to be witnessed. James spoke first. "Sir, tomorrow is Sunday. I'll need the morning off to attend church services." Mr. Gilmore looked shocked. "And the following Sunday being Easter, I'll need the entire day off so that I can be refreshed for work on Monday." James remained pleasant but assertive. Mr. Gilmore, now recovered, hesitated, nodded curtly and left. From that time on James's Sundays were free.

The walk to church was exhilarating. The service brought back lessons seldom remembered during the past year. Peace filled his spirit. His trust in God was strengthened and his outlook on life brightened. He didn't sit in one of the forward pews like he used to with his family; the back corner suited him well at this point in his life. God could hear him there also.

Easter Sunday was exactly the kind of day everyone wishes for on that occasion. His walk to the Tornsons led him westward, and in the morning sunlight, the hills were resplendent with the blooming dogwood against the dark evergreens and the new leaves of maple and elm. Whose spirit would not soar on such a wonderful morning? He carried in his hand a discarded sheet of newspaper. In his pocket was the precious letter. He stopped to pick a bouquet of wild violets for Mrs. Tornson and walked with quick light steps to the house that he had once thought would be his home for seven years.

Mrs. Tornson wept openly as she embraced him. "Oh, Yamie, I prayed dat you vould come. Ve vanted so much to see you again to say how sorry . . ."

James put his finger to his lips in a hushing motion and said, "That is past, forgiven, and forgotten. Let's be happy on this beautiful day."

"Oh yes, yes," she laughed exuberantly. "You know how ve vere alvays lazy on Sunday morning. Ve have not yet eaten breakfast, hoping dat you vould be here in time to yoin us."

"Wonderful! But I warn you, I have worked up a giant appetite walking over here."

"Goot, goot! Dat's vy I cook—so dat it vill be eaten vit pleasure." How James had missed her cheery chatter!

It was indeed a wonderful day. Mrs. Tornson accepted the flowers joyfully, but added, "Yust see vat buds are on de flowers you planted. Next veek dey vill be in full bloom."

Mr. Tornson was keenly interested in the article James read to him from the sheet of newspaper about the fact that many Germans from Pennsylvania had settled in the Shenandoah Valley. "You see, now there are Lutherans in Virginia," James told him.

Their discussion on that topic left the atmosphere between them amiable. James now asked, "Sir, I need to ask a favor of you. I have written a letter to my parents. Would you mail it for me? I have learned that the post office for overseas mail is in the shipping office near the docks."

"Yes. Yes, I know. I too inquired. I'll be happy to mail it for you. Thank you." Mr. Tornson's thanks would have seemed inappropriate to an outsider. But the man and the boy understood.

Before any of them wished it, the shadows had started to lengthen, and James took his leave with warm handshakes all around. In a dinner table prayer, Mr. Tornson had thanked God for food and friends, and for the reconciliation between God and man, and between man and man. The sweater, cleaned and repaired, kept out the evening chill as James walked.

V

EXPANDING CIRCLES

James's circle of acquaintances expanded with his regular church attendance. There were others of less prominent families who sat to the rear of the church. A balcony at the back of the building had some black slaves in attendance. However, it was said that many of them attended an outdoor service led by an itinerant preacher, if their masters did not insist on their presence at the Anglican Church.

Even the Gilmore nephew had begun warming toward him. "What do you do on Sunday afternoons?" the young man asked one day.

"Oh, I get out into the clean air, just to see the flowers blooming in the yards and feel the fresh breeze. I used to walk to the docks and watch the ships, but I don't do that anymore." He would not tell about the four-mile walk to the Tornsons which he undertook only rarely, nor the reason why ships no longer held a strong appeal for him.

"I want to go with you next Sunday afternoon. May I?"

"Would your uncle approve?" James asked in surprise.

"I hope so. I have to get away from the shop and the family for a while."

James could picture life in the big house—the Gilmores endlessly fussing over details. "We can only go with Mr. Gilmore's approval. I am fourteen. I don't know how old you are, but neither of us want to get in trouble with him."

"I am sixteen, but he doesn't give me credit for much sense. My ten year old cousin gets all the attention and privileges." James remembered the petulant girl, dressed in finery, who sometimes accompanied her mother when she brought the meals. She turned her nose up at the swarthy workroom and complained about the smells.

James had mixed emotions when Nathan Gilmore returned with the word, "He says it's all right." Those Sunday afternoon excursions had become precious to James. He wasn't sure he wanted to share them with this glum co-worker. Still, he yearned for friendship.

"Uncle Norman is starting to like you. At first he said that I should remember that you are a servant, while I am family. But he thinks now that you are trustworthy and not a bad influence. Only, he says we are not to stray too far, to be back before dark, to stay away from sailors near the waterfront, and let's see what else . . . Oh yes, to be good," Nathan said.

James stifled a sigh, thinking that he would remain on his guard and keep his private life separate from this boy who was trying to become a man against odds. Friendship would take time.

The day went better than expected. After the church service, Nathan went to the family carriage and came back with a basket of food to where James waited for him. Then they set off together to make an adventure out of a few hours of freedom on a summer day in Richmond—a new experience for Nathan.

James sensed that Mr. Gilmore was watching them closely the next day to see if the new familiarity between his nephew and his servant would affect their work efficiency. Nathan, as much in need of a friend as James, was ready to talk as they worked; but James wisely kept his responses to a minimum.

The workroom had become a more comfortable place. Mr. Gilmore relaxed his supervision a bit, at times even leaving the two boys alone at the press while he talked with other businessmen. He never stayed away long, lest an influential customer might come in during his absence.

As the city grew, so did the multiplicity of businesses. Mr. Gilmore, in distress, one day informed his workers that another printer had arrived and would be setting up shop some distance away. He did not like competition. It made him even more nervous than usual. He spent many hours thinking of a way to maintain his prominence in his field.

The arrival of the competitor had little effect at first, but months later there was a noticeable reduction of printing orders. Slyly, Mr. Gilmore sent Nathan to visit the other shop with a request for information about a possible printing job. When the lad returned he brought the answer. The competitor offered a slightly lower price.

Mr. Gilmore was too astute to succumb to waging a price war which neither of them could win. "The only way to compete is to do it better," observed Nathan. While Mr. Gilmore continued to fret, that remark came back to him repeatedly. How was it possible to do it *better*?

The answer came unexpectedly one day when a newly arrived government official entered the shop with a document to be printed. "Do you use the William Caslon type? I hope so, because this is a very special document. I've seen his work in England, and it is the very best."

Mr. Gilmore blinked. "Just what are your special requirements?" he inquired.

"Well, I like the roman type, but these key words I would like to have in italics for the proper emphasis. Can you do that?"

"How many copies do you need?"

"Eventually several thousand, but for now, I need fifty. Can you do the work?"

Mr. Gilmore was nothing if not a shrewd business man. He nodded gravely. "Unfortunately, our shipment of the Caslon type has not yet arrived. The unpredictability of shipments is a cross we have to bear here in the colonies. We shall be happy to make you the very best fifty copies possible at once and then convert to the Caslon type when it arrives."

Pleased, the customer departed. Mr. Gilmore burst into action. He would hasten to find the next ship leaving for England with a ship's officer who could hand deliver his order to the Wm. Caslon Typefoundry. Gilmore was still number one!

"It looks like your suggestion to go for quality rather than quantity should get you some respect around here," James told Nathan. The latter grinned and squared his shoulders. He was beginning to feel like a man.

At Nathan's suggestion the sign over the shop was changed to "Gilmore Quality Printing." It became known as the place for excellence. Important people were regular customers. Members of the House of Burgesses, a judge of His Majesty's court, wealthy planters—anyone who wished to make a proclamation and have it circulated among the citizenry arrived with their orders. Precision and legibility were highly valued.

The diversity of cultures in the city and throughout the colony made for a stimulating mix of ideas and languages. Variant religious ideas were often discussed in the tonsorial establishments, inns, and in the markets. A new name for the conglomeration of backgrounds was heard more frequently those days—"Americans." The name seemed to say it all for those who had come to escape poverty or prison, or to seize the opportunity to build a fortune from the virgin forests or the fertile tidelands that were rapidly being turned into productive plantations.

James was to learn about an institution that played a significant role in the life of the Virginian citizenry. On a late summer Sunday, as he approached the church, he came upon an oxcart parked around the corner from where the liveried carriage drivers usually stood waiting for their passengers. Drawing near, he nearly shouted with surprise at seeing the Tornsons, dressed in their best clothes, apparently waiting for someone.

When they saw him, Mrs. Tornson exclaimed, "Chames, we were waiting for you." He smiled at the change in her diction. "Yames" was now "Chames," and the *w*'s were no longer *v*'s. She had obviously been trying to adapt.

"This is a very important day in our lives. We are getting married soon after the service." Laughing at the astonishment on James's face, Mr. Tornson continued, "Oh, we were married all right, but not legally."

"I don't understand."

"We were married by a pastor who held services in a small church near us where we went regularly. Then when we went to get our certificate of marriage we were told that only the Anglican priest could legally perform such official acts."

Wilma chimed in, "Oh, August was so angry that we left the clerk's office and had never gone back. We didn't want to come to church here because it seemed so unfair. This was supposed to be a free country, and still they could tell us that we were not married, even when we had the statement from our pastor."

"But now, we have decided that we do want the certificate, and so we will go through the ceremony just as the law says," August added.

"And we want you to stand up with us as a witness. Will you do that?" Wilma asked.

James only had time to nod, and then the church bell rang. They hurried in and sat quietly together in a back pew. Apparently the service was not as distasteful to August as he had feared. His face grew soft with pleasure at the words that James sang at his side. His wife was humming some of the familiar melodies and moving gently with the rhythm.

The marriage ceremony was simple and soon finished since Mr. Tornson had given the necessary information beforehand. Soon they were walking away with the precious document safely tucked into his pocket.

"Come with us to the cart. We will go to our wedding dinner," Wilma said merrily. Triumphantly she pulled back the burlap cover to reveal a reed basket covered with a colorful tablecloth and a jug of apple cider.

Mr. Tornson had already picked the spot for their festive repast. The oxen were driven off the road down a path where they were tethered and allowed to eat grass. Climbing over a small knoll, the three came to a level grassy plot near a gently bubbling spring. No wedding banquet was ever held in a more gracious setting. Wilma's fried chicken, homemade cheese and bread, and the crisp apples her husband had bought for this special occasion were most satisfying.

"When this day began, I would never have dreamed this would happen," James observed.

"We have another secret. Shall we tell him, Wilma?" Mr. Tornson asked.

Wilma nodded, blushing, her eyes shining with happiness. Mr. Tornson cleared his throat and then announced, "The main reason we wanted to get our marriage certificate is that we want our child to be properly recorded."

The news brought a whoop from James. "You are going to be parents! How wonderful! Tell me, when."

"In the spring. April, maybe."

James was already envisioning a child playing around the buildings, later exploring the woods, when Mr. Tornson said, "There is one more surprise." He waited for James to show his curiosity and then added a bit more seriously, "In two weeks we are moving across the mountains into the Shenandoah Valley."

James was briefly nonplussed, but then it all made sense. Wilma would have help through her delivery and early motherhood. They would be with people from their own culture. The baby would grow up with religious training as they had.

In his happiness for them he felt a twinge of loss. These had been his first American friends. He would likely never see them again. After wishing them the best of success, he warned, "Please, don't go too far west. The French and Indians don't like anyone getting too close to the lands they call their own." His former master—so ready for adventure—could take care of of himself and his family.

Political differences became more prominent throughout the colonies. In Virginia especially, men of influence forcefully and consistently made use of the freedom to express their opinions. Justice George Farland, the judge appointed by the king to establish a court that would deal with legal problems in the Richmond area, was frequently called upon to render decisions in disputes of slander, property rights, and criminal trespass, along with rare capital offenses to be tried. Highly respected for his fairness, he took pains to have both parties understand the justice of his verdicts and to establish the rule of law in that boom town.

Judge Farland had come into Gilmore Quality Printing on numerous occasions, sometimes accompanied by his son, a slight, solemn lad about the age of James. Usually Mr. Gilmore dealt with him personally since he was a most valued customer. James heard the two men discussing a case that had stirred a great deal of controversy in the city. "Many will not agree with my ruling on this one. I need this explanation posted on every public building and along Market Street. It must be printed by Monday at ten o'clock. Will you have it ready by that time?"

"Oh, yes. We will put forth every effort, and we will not disappoint you. Your fifty copies will be ready by mid-morning Monday."

It was now Saturday afternoon. Nathan was planning on an all day fishing trip with friends Sunday. He suggested, "If I get the type all set and make a correct proof sheet, then we can close the shop until Monday morning and still finish fifty copies by ten o'clock."

After some persuasive discussion, Mr. Gilmore reluctantly agreed, but fidgeted even more than usual around his nephew as he worked. Finally he accepted the proof sheet, and after taking it and the original manuscript to his house where the light was better, he declared the proof correct and returned it to the workroom. James and Nathan were busily cleaning up the place. The proof sheet was put in a safe place for referral on Monday.

The very hazard of leaving an important piece of work to the two youngsters had given him a pounding headache, Mr. Gilmore asserted. He wouldn't feel fit to go to church on the morrow. He questioned James again about an adequate supply of ink and paper being on hand. Shortly before midnight, the lights were extinguished and the shop shut down.

Curiosity led James to the proof sheet by Sunday's early light. Judge Farland's decision dealt with a mentally deficient fifteen-year old boy accused of peeping into windows of ladies of the city. The problem was aggravated by the fact that he had actually entered the home of a prominent family who had a teenage daughter.

The city had reacted hysterically. Parents said he was a menace to their womenfolk, that he must be put away for the remainder of his life. Others called for a public punishment to teach him a lesson.

The boy had recently come to town with his single father from their home in the foothills. He was bewildered by sights he had never experienced. The masses of people confused him. He had wandered away from their rooming house when his father needed to meet buyers for the logs he had brought to town. His act of trespassing had not been done with criminal intent, nor had any harm been done except for the fear generated by his innocent but unacceptable behavior.

Therefore, Judge Farland would not impose punishment for the crime. Rather, he would counsel the boy and his father in ways to conduct themselves. They were to be released to return to their remote dwelling, and on warning of retribution by the court, no one was to harass or delay them in any way.

That was the gist of the proclamation. However, several sentences did not seem to fit the theme. The word "not" had seemingly been omitted in one instance; in another, a similar but incorrect word had been used. Nathan, with his mind on fishing and pestered by his uncle, had erred. But now he had already left for his outing.

Mr. Gilmore had kept the original script at his house. He had emphatically stated that he did not want to be disturbed on his day of rest. Still, the possibility that Judge Farland's extraordinarily humane decision might be reduced to meaningless gibberish troubled James. He needed to make a decision, though it might not be a politic one. At last he determined to do what seemed right to him and let the consequences take care of themselves.

When the church service ended, the distinguished worshippers who sat in the front pews would leave first and walk to their carriages. James slipped out as soon as the usher opened the door and waited at the carriage as the judge and his son approached. "Please, sir, excuse me for troubling you. Would you please read this proof sheet of the manuscript you brought us yesterday and see if it meets with your approval?"

Judge Farland was surprised, but took the sheet and looked it over. It seemed he was going to dismiss the request with a cursory glance, but then he spotted one error and immediately made a notation. "This correction will need to be made before more copies are done," he said emphatically.

He had still missed one sentence that did not read logically. "It will be taken care of," James promised. "Please let me know if the second sentence in the paragraph below that one is correct."

Shaking his head, Judge Farland noted the correction to be made. "Now are there any other mistakes here?" he asked, looking keenly at the boy.

"No, sir, I don't think so. Thank you very much for your time." He turned to leave.

The judge questioned, "Are you the one who set this type?"

"No, sir."

"I must commend you to Mr. Gilmore when I see him."

The boy looked alarmed. "Please don't do that, sir. Please."

"He doesn't know that you are doing this?" the judge persisted.

"No, sir. He had a very bad headache last night when he checked the proof sheet, and I knew he wouldn't be looking at it again. In fact, he is confined to his bed today. His nephew is away for the day. I would rather that they didn't know about it."

"You fear that he may dismiss you from his employe?"

A smile flickered around his lips as James replied, "Hardly, sir. I am his indentured servant."

"Well, my son George will pick up the copies promptly at ten o'clock. Can I depend on getting fifty correct copies?" The judge's penetrating gaze was fixed on the boy who thought that anyone trying to deceive him would be most unwise.

"Absolutely, sir. I'll make the corrections in the type myself before we start printing." With that he hurried home.

Mr. Gilmore staggered into the workroom the next morning, with the look of a sick man. "My head is still pounding. I can't even see straight," he moaned, "and my whole left side feels weak."

"Please don't worry yourself. Nathan and I can make these copies," James urged.

"Well, it's a good thing I read that proof sheet before my headache got this bad. I guess you two can handle the rest." Encouraged by Nathan to do so, he returned to bedrest.

When George arrived the copies were ready. "Father is so pleased that you spoke to him yesterday. He's been really troubled by this case. Now he can explain himself and maybe prevent any mob reaction."

"You can be proud of him for doing what is right, rather than bowing to popular demands," James commented. They chatted pleasantly for a while, and then George said, "I must take these to be posted before there are many people on the streets."

On the following Sunday there was a flicker of recognition between the two boys as George walked beside his father and passed the pew where James sat. A nodding acquaintance had begun.

Mr. Gilmore's condition had scarcely improved after several weeks of rest. He was lethargic, not even fretting over happenings at the shop. Nathan tried to reassure him by giving a complete report every evening, but he added, "We really should be bringing in another person to train for the work. Then you could spend more time with customers and not so much time in the workroom. With another boy like James, we could do more business."

"I doubt that there is another boy like James," Mr. Gilmore said with resignation. "But you're right. I'll see what I can do." Little by little he was loosening up on the reins—not by choice, but as his health dictated.

The new employee was a man of uncouth habits and surly manners. James was relieved to hear Nathan say, "Since you are a free man, you must find your own lodging. Included in your wages are five shillings a month for renting a room. Just be sure that you are here and ready to work at the proper time."

Nathan had sensed his friend's distaste for sharing quarters with the new man and had averted tension in the workroom. James could keep his private corner. He expressed his appreciation for the young manager's thoughtfulness. The new man gradually became more agreeable; camaraderie became more frequent.

After six months Mr. Gilmore was able to return to the shop in reasonable health. Sometimes he even complained that there were too many workers doing little, but then another order would come in to brighten his mood. He need not have worried because another solution soon presented itself.

Judge Farland's carriage drove up to the shop and the gentleman asked to speak with Mr. Gilmore, who had to be called from his living quarters next door. He arrived with his best smile to take another handsome order. Today, however, the matter of business was different.

The judge was a forthright man and came straight to the point. "I've come to buy the remaining years of indenture of the lad you have here named James."

"Oh, Your Worship, I had no plans to do that. He is well trained by this time, and I could not ask him to leave."

"You would not be dismissing him. I am asking you to let him come to us, my son and me." He mentioned an attractive price for buying out the contract, and with his authoritative air, left no doubt that he would not take a refusal lightly. Mr. Gilmore sputtered, but thought it wise not to cross so influential and loyal a customer. He called James from his work, and with only a brief explanation the transfer was made.

James's shocked surprise was mixed with trepidation. Nathan was dismayed. "I guess we'll have to get along without you. I'm glad we hired another worker, but we will miss you very much."

"You will make a great manager and I wish you well. Surely we will see each other again some time. Good-bye," James replied. Then the friends were parting with a quick handshake.

Mr. Gilmore was left muttering something about wishing he had kept his mouth shut about having too many employees when the editor brought the last copy for the newspaper. The editor was a friend of the judge, he remembered.

VI

The Cost of Friendship

Judge Farland indicated that James was to ride in the coach with him instead of with the driver. James hoped that meant that as they rode there would be an explanation of what was expected of him. During the silence that ensued, he could hardly keep from squirming. Then the judge took from his vest pocket the writ of indenture and read it. "You have three years remaining on your indenture."

"Yes, sir," was the only reply James felt appropriate.

Finally Judge Farland made his intention known. "My son, George Jr., and I noted your loyalty, intelligence, and consideration. As you know, George is about your age and has many of the privileges one hopes every young person could have. He does, however, have a deprivation that is burdensome for him. His mother died when he was six years old. I am often away from home for days at a time, so he spends much time alone or with servants. Even in school he has few friends among his peers. In fact, he is starting to hate school, although I know that he has a love of learning."

The judge had been speaking almost impersonally, looking out the carriage window at times. Now he looked earnestly at James. "James, I hope that you two will be good friends, although I understand that friendship takes time; but that is my goal. For now I'm asking you to be his companion. You will go to school with him, and I will provide your needs for school and home. What do you say?"

Too overcome to speak immediately, James tried to organize his emotions. He had learned to distrust propositions that seemed too good to be true. Still, the earnestness and kindness of his benefactor seemed unmistakable. "Master, I can't tell you how grateful I am. I really missed going to school. As for being a companion to your son, I will do the very best I can."

"I want it understood that I don't expect you to be his personal servant, doing for him what he should do for himself. He wouldn't want that either. What he needs is someone to share time, conversation, and studies with. After Sunday I'll be going to Williamsburg for three days. When I return, I hope to hear that our arrangement is working well."

With that, they were entering the driveway of Farland Estate. The room to which James was directed was not spacious but certainly superior to any he had occupied since leaving home. A *real* bed was covered with fresh linen, and a chest and wardrobe stood ready to receive his belongings—of which he had none.

That situation would soon be corrected as a tailor and seamstress arrived promptly to take measurements for several outfits of clothing. They told him that his master had arranged for him to come by their shop early in the morning for a fitting, and that they were to have one outfit completed by that evening, Saturday. The thoughtfulness with which these details had been arranged enhanced his pleasure. He determined that at the earliest possible moment he would take a thorough bath and dress in his one clean change of garments.

The carriage had left again to bring George home from school. James heard the Negro servant greet him at the door and ask of his well-being. He heard George say, "Well, I'm fine, Sam. Tomorrow there's no school and I'll be even better."

Shortly he was summoned to Judge Farland's study. The doorman, Sam, directed him to the room. He would need a guided tour to find his way around.

If George had been surprised by his father's move, he gave no indication, but James felt unsure and awkward. "I'm glad you will be living here," George said, extending his hand.

"I am very happy to be here, Master George," James replied.

"You may simply call him 'George.' We can't have him thinking of himself as a little King George," the judge asserted.

"Well, what do companions do together? What do you usually do in your free time?" asked George.

"I usually don't have much free time, but Sunday after church I used to walk in the woods and study plants or watch a spider spin its web. Not exciting, but interesting."

"Well, the woods are rather far away, and Callie and Sam are mighty hard on any spiders making webs around here," George said.

"If you don't mind, I would really like to make a tour of the premises so I won't get lost if ever left on my own."

"A great idea!" interjected the judge.

As the two left the study, James heard him tell Sam, "Tell Callie to set the table for three for dinner."

The tour completed, George, as requested, ordered a bath prepared for James, who mentally began rehearsing table manners so long unused. He felt like pinching himself to see if all this were really happening.

James sensed during dinner that the judge was discreetly watching him. "When you two are here alone you will eat together. Sometimes, after an absence, I might want to eat alone with my son. Of course, if we are having adult guests it may be that only the adults will eat in here at one time." James nodded his comprehension of the judge's wishes.

"When we eat alone, that's when I get the lectures," George said in a loud whisper that was not meant to be inaudible. Judge Farland heard, shrugged, and smiled. In a less joyous situation, James may have had a memory of his own father, but now that was obscured by the present pleasurable happenings.

The school they attended was for secondary education and had a better than normal supply of books and maps. A large slate board on the wall held the schoolmaster's instructions. Individual students carried their own small slates. A book of orthography, writing paper, quill pens, and ink completed the packet of school supplies.

As they rode to school in the carriage, George described the situation. "The schoolmaster is old Nigel Jones. The parents of the students pay his salary and he tries very hard to impress them by spouting off Latin phrases, but his teaching doesn't get across to the students. That makes him frustrated, and he starts swinging his switch, but he's careful not to hit those whose parents pay the bulk of his salary."

"Has he ever hit you?" James asked.

"No, but I know he'd like to sometimes."

They had arrived at the school and were alighting when George nodded toward two sturdy boys walking toward the building. "Those two are the Russell brothers. Their father got rich selling timber for overseas export. Now he wants his sons to become gentlemen, but they are both rude and rough and do nothing but make trouble. The schoolmaster can't discipline them because they are stronger than he is, and besides, their father is a big contributor."

As James and George started up the walk, Bruce Russell spotted them. "Hey, look, everybody," he shouted, "we have a new boy here."

The other brother, Horace, taunted, "Yeah, I'll bet George's father hired him a bodyguard. Georgie couldn't ride that carriage right into the school building, so he got a bodyguard to take care of him in school."

Like sharks smelling blood, the Russells gathered around and asked repeatedly, "Is he your bodyguard or not?"

Finally George retorted, "No, he's not. He's an indentured servant."

"Oooh, well now! A personal servant! Real high class!"

It was a relief to go through the school doors. George approached the schoolmaster to introduce James, but they had to wait while Mr. Jones finished writing a lesson on the slate board. "This is James Bankstone. My father wants him to attend classes here with me," George told him.

The pudgy, unsmiling man stared at James over his glasses, and without acknowledging the introduction asked in his raspy voice, "What grade level will you be in?"

"Sir, you see, I haven't attended classes for several years, and I'm not sure where I would fit," James answered.

"Start him at the lowest level," said George, with the good intention of helping James avoid a situation where he might not be able to do the work and would become the target of the switch. He regretted already having identified his companion as an indentured servant.

Most of the students cared little about the social status of the new boy. Obviously, he had the approval of Judge Farland or he wouldn't be here, and it was Judge Farland who was the driving force behind this school which was an experiment in public secondary education open to all those who would abide by its rules. The Russells, however, looked at James as fair game. Here was someone lower than themselves, and they would shift to him the silent ostracism they felt from their schoolmates. They assumed that skinny George would not tell on them for they had emphatically informed him of what that would mean in the estimation of his fellow students. They were more inclined toward the behavior learned in their father's lumber camp, than in learning to behave like gentlemen. Weaklings simply did not survive the initiation of the camps.

When school closed, one of them yelled for all to hear, "Look at that. He has a personal servant, and there he goes carrying his own school bag. Which one of you is the boss?"

The ride home in the carriage was silent. George knew he had disappointed his companion who was probably feeling betrayed. What should he have done, he wondered.

The next day was worse. "Now look here, fella. If you're the master, he should be carrying your books. Your father bought these clothes he's wearing and gives him food and a bed. That should be worth something to you, right? Don't be such a sissy." Thus they taunted George and ridiculed him in front of the others.

The ride home was again steeped in resentment and uncertainty. Finally James asked, "Is this why you have your driver take you to school?" He took George's silence as affirmation.

At last George spoke, "I'd like to show them that they can't bully me."

"So, shall we walk to school like the others tomorrow? Only the girls have drivers bring them some of the time."

George looked at him wide-eyed. "They would bother us even more."

"Then we will just endure it more. They'll soon tire of it," James countered.

Judge Farland returned from Williamsburg that evening. "How is it going, boys?" he asked.

"It's good to be back in school," James replied when George remained silent.

"We are going to walk to school in the morning," he finally said.

His father took this to mean that his son was showing signs of increased vigor. He had mildly objected when George asked to have the driver take him.

It didn't work out the way James had hoped. "Oh my goodness! You've had a long walk this morning. You must be tired," chided Bruce. "That's why you are going to have James carry your bag, right?"

George stood hesitant, and with supreme boldness, Horace took the bag from him and handed it to James. "Now that's better, isn't it?" When no answer was forthcoming, the question was repeated, "Isn't it?" Weakly, George nodded. Something had been started here that would be hard to stop. Indeed, it got worse over the next weeks.

James found that what little instruction he got was easily mastered, and he was left with time on his hands. He enjoyed listening to the lessons presented to the upper levels. That seemed to annoy Mr. Jones. After being told sharply to pay attention to his own lessons—even though he protested that they were already finished—James learned to keep his head down when Mr. Jones was turned facing the class, and to look up only when he wrote on the wall slate.

George, on the other hand, was enjoying freedom from harassment, and though he may have felt a twinge of guilt when he saw the bullying transferred to James, he heard repeatedly that that was the way it was supposed to be between master and servant. At least, it was an easier way.

There came a day when George was unable to complete a mathematics problem and was told to take it home on his slate and work on it. He chafed under the requirement, complaining that it didn't matter if he ever learned it. Judge Farland was again away from home or James might have refrained from remarking, "It isn't so hard if you think of it this way," and then proceeding to complete the solution. "That's the way Mr. Jones explained it," he added.

George grumbled, "I guess that was when I was sketching a castle."

James had noticed that George spent much time drawing and was very good at it. "You would have to be able to do this problem in mathematics in order to build a castle like that," he said.

"At least old Jones will let me alone when I take this to him tomorrow," said George.

The Russells had begun to feel a kinship with George during mathematics class since he, too, had difficulty. When they congratulated him on a completed lesson the next morning, he said flippantly, "Oh, I just had James do it for me."

"Really?" they asked. "He did this work? If you would make him help us like that we could get old Jones off our backs, too," Horace urged.

"Yeah, and get our old man to back off, too," said Bruce. "He really got us good with that strap of his when we took home our last report."

"You know that wouldn't be right," George protested feebly.

"Oh sure, I suppose it was right when James did *yours.* Your father would like to hear about that; so would Mr. Jones."

George knew he had erred, but what could he do? "Well, why not?" he agreed. It was such an easy solution to their problems.

More and more problems were given to James to cipher. Better and better were the grades appearing on the Russells' and George's records. James knew the scheme would be short-lived; something would have to be done. A face-to-face confrontation might get quite ugly. Simply making the scheme unprofitable might bring it to a halt, he thought, as he deliberately used a wrong procedure and ended with a wrong answer.

It made things worse. The three boys were made to come to the big slate and demonstrate the method used. It was a disaster. At last, Sarah Herndon came forward and provided the correct method and answer.

If Mr. Jones had suspicions about their past assignments, he said nothing. He wanted only to finish this day and go home to his comfortable chair and cup of hot tea. The aggravations of the profession took the pleasure out of what he had once enjoyed; but then, that was back in England where he had tutored a wealthy family's children in their home, not a primitive institution like this one. He really did not like the idea of public education.

The Russells did not take the humiliation lightly. "He did that on purpose, and we're going to make him pay," they told George.

"Anyone can make a mistake," George objected, trying to defend his companion, but he had a sinking feeling that big trouble lay ahead.

The confrontations with the Russells became increasingly harsh. "We are friends of your master," they told James. "He wants you to carry our bags, too," and they added their loads to the two he already carried. James would have refused, but since George said nothing in his defense, he decided to comply.

The schoolmaster noted the subservient role James was filling, and he also used him for his convenience. He would assign the more onerous chores to James. Soon the fetching of drinking water and firewood, washing the slate, and sweeping the room had become a part of his daily curriculum. Even so, James told himself that he was learning lessons he would otherwise have missed. He felt certain it was not what Judge Farland had intended, yet he knew how much it would hurt his master were he to relate his son's cowardice at precisely the time when the judge assumed that the arrangement was good for both of them and was keeping George interested in school?

One day as Mr. Jones wrote a problem on the wall slate, James was copying it secretively on his slate. He was sitting behind the class that was being instructed, and he felt safe from the schoolmaster's gaze. In front of him was George, supposedly writing the problem on his slate, but actually drawing an elaborate tower connected to a bridge and moat. "Now then, turn in your slates before we have our noon recess."

George paled; he had nothing but a sketch on his. In desperation, turning to James, he saw the lesson fully copied and completed. Their slates were identical. While Mr. Jones erased the wall slate, George switched slates and took James's up to the desk.

"James, turn in your slate. I want to see if you worked the problem I gave you yesterday," the schoolmaster continued.

"I worked it yesterday, but didn't think you wanted to see it; so I've erased it." James knew he couldn't tell the whole truth.

"It's time for reports, and I must let your master know what you have been doing." With that he took from James the slate with the sketches, and immediately frowned angrily. "This is what you waste your time on. Judge Farland gives you everything you need to learn and make something of yourself, and you waste his charity. You waste my time and my patience too." It was not a pretty sight as the switch was applied vehemently over James's back and shoulders. The Russells grinned at each other. James was ordered to stay in during recess.

As the students left the building to take a break in routine, Sarah walked up to George and hissed, "You are the one always drawing on your slate. I believe *you* are responsible for what happened to James. If you ever do anything like that again, I'll tell on you for sure, and I'll tell your father, too."

That evening there was no conversation between the boys. They ate their meal in silence, and James went to his room and closed the door. Both of them felt very alone.

George knew that Sarah would follow through on her threat. She was smarter than most of the boys in the classes, and she had a strong sense of fairness about her. She too was growing up without a mother, an only child, and a bit of a tomboy who wasted no time in coyness. Her father, the editor of Richmond's newspaper, was a close friend of his father. Lately she had begun paying attention to James and probably pitied him for the teasing he was getting. It was easy enough for her to stand up for him; she was just a girl, and the Russells would never bully her like they did him. No matter how he rationalized it, though, the situation was becoming more and more distasteful to him.

The Russells saw their chance to avenge the mathematics debacle by way of creating conflict between James and the schoolmaster. They approached George with a plea. "We were supposed to take some gunpowder out to the camp this week-end. We left the bag where it got rained on. Some of it had to be thrown out. Our father will nearly kill us if we come up short with his gunpowder. We know that your father keeps some on hand for his hunting. What we need is a small handful to fill up the bag he gave us. Would you please get that for us?"

The request seemed harmless enough. George really didn't want anything to do with the Russells ever again. "I'll make a bargain with you," he told them. "I'll get the gunpowder for you, but then you promise not to tell my father about the problems James has done for us." Maybe this would end their dealings, he thought.

Agreeing to that was easy enough for boys who had scarcely learned the difference between a truth and a lie. Their entire request was, in fact, a lie. They had other plans for the gunpowder. As any mischief-maker who has spent time near an open fire knows, a whole lot of excitement can be generated with a very small amount of gunpowder.

The weather had turned quite cool and James was cautioned to keep sufficient firewood on hand and to be sure that the fire was banked well before leaving the building.

The students and teacher would spend a half hour outside in the warm noon sun on most days. Horace Russell asked for permission to stay inside during the recess in order to finish a spelling assignment. The schoolmaster was surprised at the request but assented.

The lengths of firewood were piled near the hearth, and one with sections of dry loose bark was on top. It was easy to sift a bit of gunpowder down into the crevice and recover it. Horace smiled at his handiwork and then went outside saying he had finished his lesson preparation, but knowing that there would be no orthography immediately after recess this day.

"It feels like it's getting colder," Bruce said in a voice meant for the schoolmaster's ear. There was no immediate response, so Horace reinforced the observation, pretending to shiver.

"James, stoke the fire and add a log," Mr. Jones ordered.

James did as asked and had turned away from the fire when the explosion came. The Russells laughed; the girls screamed; all students jumped up from their seats and ran to the back of the room. James rushed back to put out some scattered embers that lay on the wooden floor. "What happened?" he asked.

Mr. Jones was livid. "What happened, indeed! You didn't move quite fast enough, and now you have a hole burned in your trousers. You just can't quit stirring up trouble, can you? I suppose you even stole the gunpowder from Judge Farland for this little stunt." James was still too puzzled to defend himself, and it probably wouldn't have mattered anyway. The switch was stinging his arms, neck, shoulders, chest—any place Mr. Jones could find a target for his anger.

"I'll see to it that you never do that again in my classroom." Mr. Jones barked out the words with each stroke. "When I've finished with you, you won't be able to do much of anything for days." James had turned his back and covered his face for protection. "I'm sure your master wants you to learn a lesson," the schoolmaster panted, resting momentarily, "but we won't damage his property except that which can heal itself. Take off your shirt and bend over my desk." His voice was cold with fury. He wouldn't stop until he was exhausted.

James looked him in the eye and said, "I don't know anything about any gunpowder. It must have been in the firewood."

"Over the desk. Now!" was followed by another vicious cut.

Driven to the breaking point, James grabbed the switch, broke it over his knee and walked out the door. There was no way he would take off his shirt for the others to see and ridicule, especially not the one girl who looked at him with a half smile almost every day. He looked back to see if anyone were coming after him, but seeing no one, he walked home.

Inside the classroom, the stunned students were speechless. A few inwardly cheered. The Russells asked, "Do you want us to get him for you?"

Mr. Jones recovered with an effort. "No. I'll take this to the judge. Class is dismissed for today."

Upon reaching the house, James saw that his master had returned, and his horse was being led to the stables. He debated whether or not to lay his case before him, but just then he saw Mr. Jones approaching at full gallop. James went to the stable and rubbed down his master's horse. "Sometimes I'd rather live with animals," he muttered. "They will soon send for me. I had better go to my room," he told the horse who gave him a friendly nuzzle.

In Judge Farland's study the schoolmaster blustered and raved. The judge walked over to his powder canister where it stood on a cupboard shelf. Around it was a sprinkling of spilled gunpowder. Tight-lipped, he told the schoolmaster, "I'll take care of this matter from here. I'll inform you in the morning."

James heard the schoolmaster's horse gallop away. He was about to go to his room when he heard a carriage arrive and decided to wait until it had left. He had scarcely entered his room when Sam came to summon him to the study.

Judge Farland said solemnly, "I have just heard two quite opposite stories—one from Mr. Jones, the other from Sarah Herndon. What I want from you is the whole truth."

"The whole truth is a long story," James answered.

"Then start at the beginning."

"Your son had been bullied daily by those big Russell brothers. That's why he didn't like going to school," James began.

Just then the door flew open and a white-faced George burst in. He seemed relieved that the two were talking.

"Continue, James. You'll have your turn later, George."

James told about his first day at school and the taunting about George needing a bodyguard, the revelation that he was an indentured servant, and the increasing pressure on George to exploit his advantage. "Mr. Jones had put me into the lowest level, but when they found out I could do their mathematics problems, they pushed me to do theirs for them. I gave them a wrong answer once and they were humiliated. They have wanted to get even ever since. I don't know how they got the gunpowder, but they knew that Mr. Jones always had me taking care of the water, wood, and cleaning, and that I would be blamed." He did not mention the ciphering he had done for George.

"I find some facts missing here. George, I want you to supply them. First, why was James put into the lowest level?"

"I thought it would go hard for him if he couldn't do the work in our level. I didn't know that he had learned so much."

"So then, you were trying to protect him? What about the use of James to carry loads for you and the Russells, the matter of the exchanged slates when James was punished for your drawings during class, the demand that he do your problems for you, as well as for them? Where was your concern for fairness then?" A storm of anger and disappointment was gathering in the judge's countenance.

The boys realized that Sarah had done a thorough job of spelling out the events of the past weeks. George took a deep breath and began shakily to admit the part he had played, including the hold the Russells had on him after they learned that James had worked that first problem.

"And the gunpowder?" asked his father.

"I took it from the canister yesterday evening," he said, continuing with the reason they had given for needing it. George's voice was steady now. The relief from deceit strengthened him. He was ready for the punishment his father would surely administer.

Judge Farland looked at his son sadly—so slight and sensitive, so like his artistic mother, and so untutored and untrained in the principles of manhood. Why had he not spent more time with him, set an example of daily righteousness, rather than having him hear only from others his pronouncements from the bench on matters that seemed so far removed from the boy's experiences? His son had been living in a fear that he could not or did not share with him.

Still, he was guilty of causing injury to another. Slowly, the judge rose from his chair and took his riding crop from the rack in the corner. To James he said, "You have the right to see justice done." Nodding toward George, he added, "Satisfy yourself," handing James the whip.

Remembering the tender bond between himself and his own father, James had a glimmer of understanding of the judge's pain. George had turned his back and bent to hold the edge of his father's desk. Of the three in the room, he was the most ready for the punishment to proceed.

This is not my duty, James thought. To George he said, "First, I want to ask, did you know that the gunpowder had been put into the wood?"

George shook his head. "No."

"We started walking to school to show we would not be bullied. Do you understand what happened when you gave in?"

"Yes. I took the easy way out and then couldn't change it."

James raised the whip and brought it down hard across George's back. He saw George's body twitch and then steel itself for another lash. "Multiply that by twenty or thirty, and you will understand something about justice," James said, hanging the whip back on the rack.

Facing the judge, James said, "I am satisfied." Then after a stressful pause, "May I know when I am to be sold?"

The question caught his master by surprise. "You mean that you want to leave?"

"I . . . don't know. I know only that a slave would not be allowed to take a whip to his master and remain in the household."

"Now just a minute! You are not the only one who knows about justice around here. None of what's happened is what I had planned for you. This was supposed to be a good thing for all of us. It can still be salvaged if we all try."

"Whatever you say," James said wearily.

"No. That's not good enough. We want you to want to stay. Right, George?"

"Yes, please, James. Things will be different from now on, I promise," George urged.

"Thank you," was all that James replied, but it brought a relieved smile from the others.

Jovially, the judge said, "Good, then it's settled—a new beginning," as he thumped James on the back.

The contact brought a cry from the boy. "I . . . I wasn't expecting it," he gasped.

"You are in pain, aren't you, son?" The judge's penetrating gaze was warm with sympathy. "Take off your shirt, and let's have a look." Then, remembering the schoolmaster's account of James's reaction to a similar command, he said gently, "Please, remove your shirt."

The sight made the judge wince. "What are we going to do about this, George?" More than thirty fresh raised welts testified to the vehemence of the beating.

George cringed, but he was the first to propose aid. "Callie always knew what to do when I got bruised."

"Ask her to come in," his father said.

Callie looked, and left to return with a basin of cool solution. "Thank you, Callie. That feels so good," James told her as she applied soothing wet towels to the bruised skin. Her expression was one of grim sadness.

"I suppose I know where you learned to handle problems like this," Judge Farland commented kindly. She nodded and continued applications for another fifteen minutes. She told James to call her if his back got hot again, and left.

The judge had been studying the scars on James's back. Now he took the indenture contract from his desk and read it again. "Would you like to tell me about your father?" he asked.

James re-told the story in ever greater detail as the two questioned him with great interest. "I've tried sending him a letter, but I'm not sure he ever received it. I believe he would have come by now if he had. I have wondered if my parents might have moved away from Oxford."

"We can determine that," said the judge. "I have a friend living north of London. I'll ask him to investigate and write back. Give me the details of where your father lived, worked, and other assignments he may have had. Better still, you write to your parents, and if he finds them, he can hand-deliver your letter also. Nothing would make them happier."

James was overcome with gratitude, excitement, relief. He wouldn't need Callie's ministrations any more that day. He had a letter to write.

Judge Farland had another letter to write also, this one to the schoolmaster. At breakfast he handed it to James. "This assures that you will receive the same treatment as if you were my son. Both of you will do your share, but no more than that, of wood and water fetching, along with the other students. I am the only one who bought your indentures. If there is anyone who doesn't understand that I want you to tell me about it. You are to be placed in the same level with George and receive all the benefits of instruction due you."

He looked earnestly at James. "This calls for a drastic change of action on Mr. Jones's part. Whether or not he can still maintain control of discipline in the classroom depends largely on your attitude when you give him this."

"I think you are asking me not to be a smart aleck," James surmised.

"Something like that, yes."

"That won't be a problem. I have had a lot of practice in humility," James assured him.

"You handle it well, but I still wouldn't provide him with a new switch if I were you," Judge Farland said with a smile.

George came to the table looking subdued but calm. He and his father had had a long, serious, heart-warming talk the night before. Breakfast was relaxed, satisfying, amiable. It would be a good day.

Mr. Jones read the note twice, and then put it in his pocket without a word. When George's class was called up to the front for recitation, James remained seated until Mr. Jones called him to come forward also. This gesture of waiting for the schoolmaster's command seemed to strike a chord of respect, and James began enjoying a more cordial relationship with him.

The Russells too sensed that their game was over. They had called to George the next morning, "Hey, what happened to your bodyguard when you got home?" George had replied, "I got whipped, and he got promoted to friend," as he and James entered together.

Again, James thought more often of his parents. What would be their reaction? How soon might he expect to see his father? It might take over two months for the letter to reach England and that long for a return, if his parents could be located. If not . . . he wouldn't think about that. In the meantime, his life was moving happily along.

It was his best Christmas in the New World. After religious services, the Farland house was alive with visitors and parties. Wonderful food such as he hadn't tasted in years appeared almost daily at mealtime, and at tea there were delicious pastries. James and George stayed mostly in the background when visitors were present. It was more fun that way.

George provided his friend with introductory comments as they watched from his bedroom window the arrival of the gentlemen and ladies in their finery. "That's the Widow Martens. She has her cap set for my father."

"Is he interested in her?"

"I don't think so. I hope not. She is wealthy, inherited a plantation, but Father doesn't need that. . . . There is John Henry. He is the justice in the next county."

There were also days when they were left alone as Judge Farland attended a ball at the governor's mansion in Williamsburg at New Year. "Let's go see how the slaves are celebrating," James proposed one afternoon.

There was joy here, too. The field workers had the week off and were playing games, singing, and telling jokes. The domestic help enjoyed the days when they were not involved in entertaining. The judge had been generous in his gifts and extra food supplies. "My father wants all of them to be happy," George said.

James saw them in a somewhat different light. "I'll wager that any one of them would trade that happiness for freedom," he replied.

George took exception to the comment. "They would never be able to cope with the strain of staying alive here. They need someone to look after them. I admit their work is often hard, but for that they are well taken care of."

James was tempted to put the question to any of the folks around them, but an honest answer would not likely be forthcoming. "Has anyone ever asked them?" he countered.

"Of course not. That's not how things work here."

"If you were in their place, what would your feelings be?" James persisted.

"How should I know?" George retorted. "Come on, let's go horseback riding."

James had to be content with planting a question in the mind of his friend. In his own mind he had grave misgivings about the matter of slavery.

In late April came a ship from England carrying a letter for Judge Farland. He brought it home and summoned James. "This portion will interest you."

James could hardly keep his hands from shaking as he read: "With regard to the search for a Dr. James Bankstone, Sr., I inquired diligently among the colleges of science at Oxford. A botanist by that name had lectured there up until three years ago. He was well respected among his peers and especially admired by his students, for he not only taught them in an interesting fashion, but challenged them to do research on their own, inspiring them to discover beneficial uses for plants. He had been commissioned by His Majesty's Minister of Commerce to study the shipping of imports from India, chiefly tea and cotton, which often arrived at our ports in less than excellent condition.

"I spoke to a former colleague who told of a great tragedy in the life of the good professor. His only son had seemingly drowned, although his body had never been found. After becoming a widower as well, he apparently lost interest in teaching. (At this, a moan escaped James's lips, but he continued reading.) The following year, he left the University and sailed for India. His work there has produced great improvements in the quality of imported cotton, as well as tea. Reports told of his work in improving irrigation methods and agriculture. However, in the past year there has been no word received from him; so his whereabouts are unknown at present.

"I have left the letter you enclosed with the colleague who will deliver it in the event Dr. Bankstone returns."

His eyes were misty as James handed the letter back to the judge. "She must have died of a broken heart," he said tremulously. "May I be excused, sir?"

He wanted to cry in the privacy of his room, but tears would not come yet. He lay on his bed staring at the ceiling unable to arrange his thoughts into any semblance of coherence.

The judge picked up the letter and read again, "'After becoming a widower . . .'—I didn't even notice that, but he did. He knows now that his mother is dead and his father may be somewhere beyond reach, if alive at all. That's not the happy ending we hoped for."

"He was hoping that his father would come and buy his freedom, Father. We can do something about that, can't we?"

"Yes. Yes, we can, but should we? Where would he go but on a fruitless chase? Give him a little more time by himself and then we'll discuss it with him."

When dinner time approached and James still hadn't come out of his room, George went in. Tears had finally come, but little consolation. "It's all my fault. If I had only gone to him that morning in Liverpool to get his permission before I went on that ship, we would still all be together. Now, I can't even ask their pardon."

"But if you could, you know they would give it whole-heartedly. Look, if you could forgive a hypocrite like me, certainly your father would forgive you. Besides, think how boring my life would have been if I had never met you." With these and other genial jibes, George talked his friend into a weak smile, and later into the walk to the dinner table. Conversation was scant but warm, and James concluded that he still had much for which to be thankful. He would survive.

After the meal they went to the study. "We have to talk about your future, James. You have two more years on your indentures. I could release you from that, but I'm afraid that you would exhaust yourself in a search, and you are still only seventeen. Apparently your home in Oxford has been sold. I think it wiser that you remain here with us, providing of course that you are free to leave at such time that you have a place to go. Can you be content with that arrangement?"

"You have both been so very kind and very . . . dear . . . to me. Thank you for asking me to stay and for all your efforts to help me." James knew that for now this was the place for him.

VII

Building Begun

In another month school had closed for the summer. There was little to occupy the boys' time. James frequently went to the stables or the tobacco drying sheds to lend a hand and feel useful. He wondered what his father would think of tobacco—the plant that people smoked instead of eating. Were plant products ever meant to be taken into the lungs instead of the stomach? Now there was a philosophical question, as well as a physiological one, he mused.

He found George with numerous sketches of buildings, bridges, and machines scattered over his bed and George himself looking bored and languid. "You'd have more fun drawing something you would actually build," James told him.

"That's not likely to happen."

"Oh, why not? We could pretend to be pioneers and build a log cabin on the farthest edge of your father's property. We'd be real settlers, and even have our own hide-out."

"Hey, that's right! What a great idea! I wonder if Father would let us buy lumber?" George said.

"We don't have to buy lumber—just chop down some trees and put them together."

"Wow, that sounds like a lot of work!"

"Think of the muscles we'd have—bigger than the Russells. All we need is two axes and your plans," James coaxed.

His friend's enthusiasm was contagious, and George decided that if this could be done, then he too could do it. He sought his father's permission. "I have a great deal of respect for people who are so resourceful that they can build their own homes with the materials from their own land. From such folks a nation is built. If you start this, though, you must finish it the best you can. If it's not finished by the time school resumes, you need to work at it on Saturdays," was the judge's reply.

It was to be the most memorable summer of their young lives. They talked into the night, planning how to proceed. The next morning they were up early, getting their horses from the stable, thanking Callie for the lunch she had packed for them, and riding off into the woods. They had decided that first they must find a suitable spot by inspecting the entire acreage.

With Judge Farland's appointment as the justice of the city of Richmond, and of Henrico and Chesterfield Counties (whose boundaries the city straddled) had come the awarding of 3000 acres of land adjoining the city to the west. The judge preferred to keep the woods intact and enjoy them in hunting. His wife had reveled in their beauty, especially in the spring.

The first argument arose over the choice of a site. George wanted to build on the highest spot; James said it would have to be near a brook or spring for a water supply. George proposed clearing all the trees toward the stream for an unobstructed view; James insisted that some would have to remain to prevent soil erosion.

Compromise and respect for each other's opinions were two of the biggest lessons learned.

When the felling of trees began, James cautioned his friend against overdoing it the first few days, but George was eager to begin on the building he had envisioned. They were both glad for the day of rest, church, and quiet activities, but eager to go again on Monday. It was George who planned the structure, and James who taught him how to cut the notches and fit the logs together.

By the end of August the walls were up, the roof on, and their muscles hard and bulging. Callie said she had never seen two boys eat like they did. As for the boys, they couldn't remember when they had felt or slept so well. The judge saw his son developing into a man and congratulated himself for bringing the two boys together.

Then one evening George told his father, "I know now what I would like to be—a builder, making things with my own hands . . . and my mind, planning and designing what I build. It's just the greatest feeling."

"You mean you want to be an architect?"

"Yes, Father. There's no limit to what a person can build—homes, churches, factories, ships, bridges."

"You are not interested in the land then?"

"Not for plundering the forest to plant more and more tobacco. We can keep the woods and use only some for lumber, and just enjoy the rest."

"I think I like that," his father said thoughtfully. "You know, of course, that an architect must study his craft, must learn mathematics, know his building materials, and likely be a student of one of the masters in order to be really good."

"Father, I have so many dreams. I want to be the very best I can."

"You have one more year in preparatory school, and then you can start on your career. Learn all you can now. Then you will do well when you get to the meat of your career studies." George heard him eagerly.

"And what would you like to do in your manhood, James?" asked the judge.

The question caught him by surprise. "I . . . I hardly know, sir. I like working with the land, with plants and animals, but I also like languages, literature, and history as much or more. Maybe I could teach. I really hadn't thought about it yet, sir," James replied, feeling a bit lost.

The judge smiled and he too began making plans and dreaming dreams for these two stalwart young men at his table.

Mr. Jones seemed calmer as the school term began. The Russells had not enrolled. Some of his students had matured during the summer and took more kindly to instruction. Maybe this would be a better year. Grudgingly at first, and then freely, he admitted to himself that James was a good pupil—one who shared his own love for Latin and history. The boy's natural curiosity was stimulated by the extra challenges given him, such as would have elicited grumbling from a lesser learner.

The boys still had work to do at the cabin to apply mortar between the logs, cover the windows with hinged sashes, and smooth the rough-hewn logs of the floor. Sawing had been a big challenge, but the boys were determined to do it by themselves.

By November it was done, although George vowed there would be improvements in the spring. "Father, why don't you bring your gun, shoot a turkey or deer, and we'll cook it in our hearth? We can all have a feast of thanksgiving."

The meal was not the culinary best Judge Farland had ever eaten, but it was the most gratifying. He was pleased to be invited to their cabin since he had not interfered during the building and was curious to see their handiwork. They were pleased that the structure was sound; no cold winds came through the walls; the roof did not leak; the fireplace worked. The judge was particularly happy to discover his son's talent and note the new purpose it gave to his life.

The school year had again come to a close, and the boys were wondering what to do with their time, when Judge Farland called them into his study. "Son, I've been thinking of your ambition to become an architect. There seems to be very little in the colonies to prepare you for the high expectations we both have. I have contacted your mother's brother in England who is willing to introduce you to the best masters there. You could study under them for two or three years and come back as one of the best."

He watched for George's expression of interest, but the boy was still too stunned to grasp its full import. "You should be in a position to make a real contribution to the development of the profession here. You would be a builder in more ways than one. That would please me much more than having you be a so-called 'gentleman,' making little if any contribution to this new land. People who only take and never give anything back are hurting themselves and everyone else. I was so proud of you when you said you wanted to be a builder."

"Oh, Father, I had no idea that would be possible. I want so much to learn, but the idea of leaving you and home frightens me."

"I know. It makes me uneasy, too. It doesn't seem possible that you have grown up so quickly; but you have, you know."

"Can James come with me?" George asked his father.

"No, I need James here."

James, too, was surprised. He had thought he would be going to England as soon as he had served his time and earned enough money for his passage. Now it was George who would be going, and he would be staying with George's father.

"James, I sorely need someone to manage the land for me. We need to bring more land under cultivation and run the entire operation more efficiently. I'm expected to get much of my income from it. Now with George studying overseas I'll need more income for his support. I want you to know that I have asked my friend in London to continue to make inquiries about your father. If there is any word about him, we will act on it as soon as possible, but for the time being, I'm asking you to be the manager of this estate. What do you say?" The judge's keen eyes studied him.

"Do you really think that I am grown up enough for that responsibility?" James remonstrated.

"I've been watching you. You take a real interest in what goes on here. The servants respect you, and you have a good practical bent about you."

The boys had dozens of questions. The judge had answers for most of them. Those that could not be answered were left to the providence of God.

Preparations began almost immediately. As the time for George's departure drew near, apprehension gave way to excitement. James warned him about seasickness, the crowded cities, and pickpockets, but assured him that he would conquer all of these.

"It's almost like we are trading places, isn't it? My father knows I'm not interested in farming. I'm so glad that you will be here with him while I'm away. When I come back it will be your turn to do whatever you wish, I promise."

"Don't pity me," James replied. "I love this land. There is so much opportunity here for people who have had so little of it. People want to be independent and work out their own future. The fairness which your father promotes will really make this a great country. Since I can't be with my family, this is the best place for me." George was relieved that they would part without rancor.

The first letter from George expressed a bit of homesickness but a lot of enthusiasm. Judge Farland was greatly relieved to learn of his son's safe arrival and the ease with which his plans were coming to fruition.

James had turned his attention to improving the economy of the estate. The problem, he decided, was that it served more as a recreational facility than a working farm. Judge Farland enjoyed bringing his friends for an occasional hunt or horseback ride, but none of this produced income. Instead of the stables only, other outbuildings should be added, the number of livestock increased, and the newly cleared land devoted to the production of crops other than tobacco, namely wheat and corn. He outlined step by step plans so that the cost of each improvement would boost the income enough to make the next step feasible.

Another proposition was that 40 to 160 acres could be rented to good farmers who would pay their rent with a share of the crops. "I'm skeptical of that," the judge protested. "I hear many cases in court because of disputes between landlord and tenant. In some cases the landlord is too greedy; sometimes the tenant is slothful and incompetent. People around here still talk about the Bacon rebellion that brought bloodshed, and wounds that are even now not healed. Class wars are very destructive."

James remembered studying about the Bacon rebellion. Small farmers had been disenfranchised by a corrupt political machine backed by the wealthiest landowners. Heavy taxes and increased freight rates had forced many to lose their livelihood, while their assessments were being used to build up Jamestown. Nathaniel Bacon had led an armed rebellion that forced new elections and restored the vote to all adult males.

"Your arrangement could be a model for land use, just as your court is for law administration," James urged. "To avoid getting lazy tenants, you could even begin by using indentured servants. By the time a man or a couple had worked for you a number of years, you would know their character, and would not be faced with the difficulty of getting them off your land if they prove incompetent. It would provide those completing their indentures with a home to look forward to."

"I never thought I would hear you promoting indentured servitude," was the judge's comment.

"If it is entered willingly and the terms are just, then it is a great opportunity. Fairness and opportunity are the keys in my opinion."

James knew he had made his point when the judge nodded. "Young man, you have just increased your responsibilities here. Now you must find me the right people."

"Oh, but sir, that means going to the auction with money to buy, unless you find a good contract to buy from a previous owner."

"That's right," said the judge. "When you are ready for that step, let me know so I can give you the money." Seeing James's reluctance he explained further. "I am not comfortable at all with the institution of slavery. It has so much potential for abuse. God can not be pleased with the brutality to a fellow man and the deprivation of his dignity that is inherent in it. I feel that the Negro, too, should be offered a choice for freedom after serving faithfully for a number of years. Not many of our citizens agree with me, since they see it as a means of cheap labor unending—one that feeds their greed. It cheapens all of us. If you can find those deserving persons then we will offer them a fair opportunity, but I will not be seen taking part in the auctioning of human chattel. Even though I have slaves, I know that I must try to do something to correct the entire situation."

James's admiration of his master escalated. He understood the need of all men for dignity and hope. Although much had been neglected at the estate due to the absence of managerial leadership, the workers seemed to welcome a work schedule that allowed for accomplishments for each day. A half day of rest on Saturday and all of Sunday was allowed, but there were to be no more days of complete idleness.

James learned that the best time to buy indentures was in the fall since most owners did not want to feed workers through the winter unless they were skilled artisans. The cost of unskilled workers' contracts was cheap and the supply plentiful as most shippers tried to complete their deliveries before winter. He had attended several auctions before he settled on a couple in their late thirties who, he felt intuitively, would be conscientious workers. They responded eagerly to his explanation of their duties—his pertaining to a corner of the estate that was to be cleared of most of the trees, and the land sowed in wheat and some fruit trees. Her responsibilities they would discuss more fully as they rode home together in the wagon. Their contracts were for four years each.

Luke and Bessie Fairbairn were sturdy and thrifty Scottish folk, highly principled, motivated, and poor. Bessie knew the art of weaving homespun material suitable for work clothing, as well as the method of preserving root vegetables for winter use, and drying apples. James encouraged them to tell of the contributions they could make by their labors and assured them that they would be appreciated. They would live in a small bungalow built by the field workers during their slack time. There was basic furniture, but they were free to add other furnishings of their own making as they wished.

By the time they had reached the estate, Bessie had expressed her readiness to take responsibility for the garden and its produce, as well as the curing of meat and making sausage. James urged her to teach her skills to Tildy, Joe's wife, the most recent Negro arrivals. The Fairbairns were introduced to Callie, whom she would help in the kitchen when necessary to entertain guests. They would get their food supplies form the main kitchen where they were stored, and prepare meals for themselves in their bungalow. It was obvious that this greatly relieved Luke who was less sociable than Bessie. He understood that Tildy cooked for the Negroes and Callie for the master. Now he and his wife would have their own privacy.

James felt that the implementation of his plan had gone rather well. Callie may have already anticipated that she would have to spare them some utensils. She accepted it with her usual equanimity. Judge Farland would meet the newcomers eventually, but he left all details of operation to James.

The judge had turned more and more to his peers for companionship during his son's absence. Sometimes James was invited to join the dinner fellowship, but more often, when there was a guest, he was happy to eat in Callie's kitchen after he had finished his work. A frequent guest was Mr. Herndon. He and the judge held long discussions about the trend of politics and society in the colony as well as the decline of commitment in the church. Too many people were substituting their love for spiritual values with material ones, they agreed. James enjoyed listening, but sometimes found himself wondering what Sarah might be doing alone at home.

On numerous occasions the Anglican priest would be absent from services on Sunday. Mr. Herndon explained to the congregation that the arrival of so many settlers caused a shortage of ministers in the outlying areas. They would be sharing their minister with some of those smaller churches. Lay ministers would read the scriptures, present a lesson, and lead the service. Mr. Herndon was chosen unanimously to serve as lay minister. Marriages, baptisms, and the Lord's Supper would be scheduled for the times when the priest would be present. A lay minister would conduct a funeral if the priest was not available. There was some murmuring about this arrangement, but it was accepted as the best possible choice as a concession to the necessities of colonial life.

Spring returned and James was eager to implement the plans for the estate which was becoming more and more of a farm. In June his contract of indenture would be complete. He had little time to wonder what would follow.

Judge Farland did not forget the occasion. He presented James with a New Testament that he would treasure always. "You are entirely free to leave. I have put aside a stipend of ten shillings per month for the three years that you have been with us, and it is now yours to do with as you wish." This was a happy surprise. His years with Farlands had been years of growth and learning. Justice Farland was the man he most admired and loved in the whole world, and the fondness was reciprocated.

Without a moment's hesitation, he acquiesced when the judge offered, "If you will stay with me and continue as you have, you will be paid a monthly salary in addition to your sustenance. You will be free to go when you desire, but I would expect due notice of your intention. When George returns, we will bring him into the arrangement and make any necessary adjustments. Agreed?" The two men shook hands and sealed the bargain. James was two months shy of his twentieth birthday.

November brought severe weather. The workers were told to repair and refurbish their cabins as much as they could. No one was to be idle long. James visited the buildings daily, criticizing where needed, and commending where warranted. He wished that he had thought earlier of a plan to offer reading classes for such times. Now that would have to wait.

Judge Farland had been called to a meeting with the governor in Williamsburg and would have to brave thunderstorms to keep the appointment. He was joined by Justice Henry, and the two set out wearing such protective raingear as they could find. The skies cleared in time for their return. The bright sunshine seemed to promise a pleasant boat ride home, but heavy coats were still needed.

The trip upstream was never easy, as the boat had to be propelled by poling. The boatmen struggled valiantly against the current. Not knowing of the downpours in the mountains a few days earlier, they had not counted on the river being so turbulent, nor so littered with debris. It was getting dark and only little headway had been made. It would be necessary to pull over to the shore and find such shelter as they could for the night. They all agreed that it would be an unpleasant night, but that was better than continuing into danger. Roads were still impassable.

Then disaster struck. The boat hit a tangle of underwater debris and capsized in an instant. Justice Henry was thrown out and made it to shore. The boatmen waded back into the water searching for Judge Farland but found no trace. Their boat remained snagged, overturned on the debris.

At first light the boatmen made another attempt to right their boat. To their utter disbelief, they found Judge Farland. His left arm, enmeshed in wreckage, was pinned behind him. His right arm lay broken against a seat with the tail of his coat tangled around it like a splint. The buttons over the chest still held closed. The coat pulled up under his right armpit had supported his head and shoulders in the air space above the water. He had a large bruise over the right temple and had been unconscious for a time. His color was cyanotic, and he coughed frequently in an attempt to clear his lungs of water he had sucked in during an effort to free himself.

The crest of the flood had now passed and progress was easier. In great urgency the men propelled the boat as quickly as possible. The judge faded in and out of consciousness.

It was early afternoon when they reached the dock in Richmond. News of the accident spread rapidly. A carriage arrived to carry the men to Farland Estates. "Stop at the pharmacy," said Justice Henry. "This man needs medicine."

The pharmacist had a different priority. "Take him home and get him into a warm bed immediately. Try to get him to drink hot liquids. I'll bring the medicine as soon as I have it prepared." The carriage sped away and the judge was soon in his own home.

James and Sam stripped off the soggy clothes, rubbed the bluish limbs under the woolen bedcovers, looked at each other in alarm, and prayed silently. The medicine arrived and relieved the coughing somewhat, but the breath sounds continued to rattle. Mr. Herndon came to see his friend and left with somber misgivings. Justice Henry would spend the night; and then outfitted with clean, dry clothes, return to his wife and young son, Patrick.

By morning the judge's body had warmed to seemingly normal temperature; but the relief was short-lived, for the temperature continued to rise to fever level. James sponged his face, arms, and chest with cool water in an effort to control the fever. There were brief periods of lucidity when the judge would try to speak, but the words were unintelligible. Throughout the day and into the night, the servants who loved him so dearly were at his side. Shortly after midnight, Judge Farland died.

No last wishes had been uttered; no provisions made for contacting his son. The grim reaper had silenced forever a powerful voice for progress and justice in the colony of Virginia. James stumbled to the door and sent a messenger to notify Mr. Herndon.

The Richmond newspaper carried on its front page the story of Justice Farland's death, but few people saw it in time to attend the funeral. A few friends, whom Mr. Herndon contacted through messengers, were present at the church cemetery as the body of their beloved friend and mentor was laid to rest. The minister was present, but it was Mr. Herndon who, through deep emotion, provided the greatest comfort. "He trusted in God. He rests in God's hands. We loved him and we miss him, but we shall meet again. Farewell, dear friend." James noted that he was not the only one who could not hold back tears.

The friends returned with James to the house. Awkwardly, they sat in the large living room, trying to make small talk. Callie and Bessie came with trays of scones and sliced apples and steaming cups of tea. They would all remember the hospitality they had enjoyed there in happier days. Sarah was there, too, and touched his arm in sympathy.

James could not bring himself to stand in his master's place at the doorway to thank the departing guests. Mr. Herndon did that, while James stood at the end of the walk and ordered the carriages brought around. At last only the two remained. "Will you come into the study with me? I need to find George's last address," James requested. He wrote the address on an envelope, and took writing materials with him, closing the door behind him, not to open it again for many days.

"James, there will be many details to take care of. I will write to Governor Burwell. I believe that this estate was awarded to George—Judge Farland—in perpetuity, and that the appointment of a new judge will have no effect on your work here." James stared in dismay. He had not even considered that possibility. "Please, don't worry. I feel sure that, in view of his excellent service, there will be no problem," Mr. Herndon said, "since there is an heir."

The most difficult day James had lived since his arrival in the New World ended with his writing to his friend George. He made no mention of what had concerned Mr. Herndon. The tragedy of losing his father would be devastating in itself for George.

It was the following week when Mr. Herndon brought a letter from the governor expressing his condolences and affirming that the estate would remain in the Farland family. He stated also that henceforth, Chesterfield County, Henrico County, and the city of Richmond would each have their own justices as the population growth demanded it. The letter closed with lavish compliments on the judge's service. "George will treasure this," James told Mr. Herndon, who then gave it to him for safekeeping.

"How are you situated financially?" Mr. Herndon asked.

"We have tobacco ready for sale and wheat ready for the grist mill. With money from that and the produce from the farm there is enough to keep going."

"Good! If you are ever in need of assistance I want to help. Just ask." With that James was left alone—with 3000 acres, eight Negro slaves, and two indentured servants.

He couldn't afford to be overwhelmed. He must remain calm, carrying on business as usual. He drove himself to work tirelessly. He involved himself in every farming operation. None of the servants could or did question his authority. He worked as hard as any of them, but they respected him, and he them.

The day George's letter arrived, James locked himself in his room and let the grief wounds flow as he read his friend's sorrowful reply. Losing a loved one when knowing that death is imminent is painful; but hearing that his robust, caring, vital father had died suddenly without his being there was crushing for George. It was plain that the letter had been written in installments interspersed with tears.

The letter ended: "Since it is now more than two months since my father's funeral, does it serve any purpose for me to come home? If you were not there, dear friend, I would already be on my way. However, Father had written how well you were doing. That would not be improved by my return.

"I must confess that I selfishly want very much to finish this course of study. I have been on location, actually supervising the construction of a building I designed. I'm eager to tell you about it, but it would be too lengthy. If I were to leave now, I would be missing the most enriching part of my training. I truly believe my father would want me to stay.

"It was a pleasure to meet relatives from my mother's side. Father never told me that my grandmother was Italian. I have been invited to visit Italy before I return.

"Oh, James, there is so much to be said; this letter cannot contain it. I'm asking you frankly, will you continue as you have been, so that I may finish my studies here? You will be well rewarded when I return. What do you say?"

"What do you say?" James repeated. Judge Farland had used that expression often when making a proposal. It made the order seem less dictatorial. James had never refused the father; he would not refuse the son now.

With the heir's permission to continue as manager, James reentered the judge's study. He wondered if there was any method for reporting income. Was there a statement of their spoken agreement on general policy of managing the farm and servants? Was there a written notice of a stipend saved for him? If so, he did not find it in a casual search. Not wishing to intrude into the family's privacy, he determined to run the farm on a pay-as-you-go basis, assuming the pressure of making each season a profitable one. The study door was closed again.

His next letter to George conveyed congratulations for his friend's achievement, as well as his own consent to remain as manager. Then he continued, "When your father asked me to begin this job, he said I had a 'practical bent.' It is in the interest of practicality that I call this to your attention. Your father died without the ability to express any last wishes, and as nearly as I can determine, leaving no will."

He then explained the plans for the use of the land, the judge's beliefs about slavery, the mention of the stipend and the monthly salary offered. He requested validation of the judge's wishes, stating that he would not seek access to any funds until George himself would return.

The letter was cordially answered with a statement that the judge's mentioned wishes were to be carried out. It bore the signature of two witnesses, one of them George's uncle.

The letter continued, "As you know, I have completed nearly two years here—the minimum length of time originally intended. Now I have a wonderful opportunity to study in Italy. My uncle would take me there, as he has long wished to visit his mother's birthplace. Many of the greatest architects of all time have their works in Italy. Please say that you will extend your service another twelve months until I return. I owe you so much.

"Your true friend, George."

What could he say? James had no reason to refuse. It was wonderful security to have George's wishes in writing. He was able to continue his job with less tension. He would still be strictly accountable for his stewardship, but he would feel free to carry out long-range plans, and to reward the servants according to their faithfulness. He would ease up on himself, too, and take time to read in the judge's substantial library. Law was an absorbing subject, but of greater interest were the literary classics. "I'm going to school right here on the farm," he told himself.

By the time George was due to return, policies had been put into effect that reflected Judge Farland's beneficent wishes. There were now two indentured couples and one single man. The Fairbairns had been informed that during their last year of indenture they would have, besides Sunday, another free day per week in which to work at building a cabin for themselves on the land he had cleared. After that they could begin renting the hundred acres. Two thirds of all crops and livestock sales would be theirs to keep. Bessie was elated. "Oh, Luke, we won't have to go looking for a home. We'll have one."

"But it won't be our land, Bessie. I want us to have our own land."

"We can save for buying our own. That's much better than being set adrift penniless when our contract is completed." Even dour Luke had to agree, and Bessie's yearning for a home would not be stifled.

With a view to future prospects, the second couple worked with greater enthusiasm. James had emphasized that only industrious workers would be considered as renters. Pete and Martha Langford were Welsh. Their hopes of breaking out of abject poverty had also brought them to America. Another portion of woods would be cleared by Pete. Martha and Tildy would keep a supply of homespun cloth on hand which they would make into work clothes. Bessie agreed to Martha's suggestion of planting plum trees and grape vines along the edge of the garden which grew larger each year. Martha had a great "receipt" for plum pudding and for preserves, she declared.

Tildy was glad to learn new skills. She had worked with Joe in the fields before, but now, with their new baby boy, it was good to be able to care for him in their own little cabin. For the first few months she had taken her spinning wheel right near his crib. The sound of it was soothing, and he slept soundly.

Charles Burton, newly arrived from England, made it a point to inform James that he had left a fiancee back home. Already he had an eye toward improving his status.

Hope was the ingredient that added zest to the lives of all. It improved their morale and their efficiency and made James's task more pleasant. The Negroes too were to have opportunity. Judge Farland had explained to James that when the first slaves were brought to America, their status was that of indentured servants who would be freed after seven years of service. Some of these had become independent farmers, artisans, and tradesmen. Had their migration been voluntary and their service equitable, there would not now be the disgraceful, divisive blot of life-long slavery in this new country.

From Sam, James ascertained that Ned had served over seven years. He was given the choice of leaving as a free man or remaining as a paid worker. Seeing him leave with his clothes and stake of five pounds in hand, clutching his emancipation papers, Sam commented, "He never mixed with the others much."

When James asked why, Sam explained that Ned had been very rebellious when his former owner bought him at an auction of slaves from Africa. His master was a religious zealot who said that bringing slaves from Africa was God's way of Christianizing them. He had insisted that all his slaves be baptized and attend preaching. Ned had learned the language well, but when he was told to be baptized, he refused. After being flogged several times, Ned would only say, "Allah is God; Allah is great." That had only infuriated his master more. One day the preacher appealed to Judge Farland saying that such was not a way to save souls. The judge agreed, bought Ned, and gave orders that Ned was not to be pressured.

"Did he ever accept baptism?" James wanted to know.

Sam shook his head. "He listened to Callie teachin' him, but he said he'd never be baptized as long as he was a slave."

"What do you think he will do now?"

Sam shrugged. "God knows."

When questioned about her choice, Callie said, "If I thought I could find the children taken from me fifteen years ago, I would go in a minute, but I don't know where to start looking. If only I could stay with young Master George when I'm too old to work, that would be my wish. This is the best home I have ever had."

"I'll record your wishes, and I think Master George will guarantee it," James promised.

Sam, already gray and wrinkled, said, "Jes' let me die here and bury me in the woods there." So it was that a small plot was designated as a final resting place. As the one who had been with Judge Farland the longest, he supplied the information to determine the dates when the others were due their offer of freedom.

VIII

The Master Returns

James awaited George's arrival but had not yet heard of the ship's sighting. It should be any day now. The anticipation was almost unbearable. He had planned to take the carriage and wait for him at the dock. Instead, George came galloping at full speed on a horse he had rented as soon as he could leave the ship.

The young men shook hands. Then, throwing aside restraint, they hugged, backed away to look at each other, and hugged again. Three years had matured both of them into confident, clear-eyed men of vision and purpose.

Eagerly James showed George the innovations he had made. They rode on horseback over the estate. "These three plots are now coming under cultivation, and because they will be rental property, you will be getting income from them without the need of supervising them. I remember how you loved to get out into the soil," James teased.

"But what about the woods Father loved so much?"

"There are still more than a thousand acres of woods untouched right along the feeder streams. By the way, our cabin still stands, and there is still virgin forest all the way from it to the main house. We can still pretend to be pioneers—you know, 'builders of the nation.'"

George was very quiet, seemingly lost in thought. When asked if he approved of the changes, he replied, "Oh, yes, of course. It takes a big load off my mind. I had been wondering what to do about all this land."

"You see," James went on, "the cultivated part is along the main stream at the back and left of the property, with plenty of room for expansion. If you should ever decide to sell off part of it, you would not disturb the appearance of your home and the woods around it. Also, the main stream along the rental property could have some of the rocks removed to deepen it, and then it could be used for floating rafts of produce to the docks."

"Father was right," George stated. "You do have a practical bent about you."

They returned to the house and enjoyed glasses of apple cider that Callie brought to them on the veranda. Sam and Callie had greeted George with genuine affection upon his arrival. It was apparent from the way they observed him from the background that they just enjoyed watching him.

James told of Ned's emancipation. Pointing to a shaded area at the edge of the woods, James said, "Sam wants to stay and to be buried there. We've built a rail fence around it to reserve it."

George nodded. "Sam is the one whom Father purchased from a hard-hearted planter. Sam had left the plantation one Sunday without permission, feeling sure that it would not be granted anyway, to visit his ten-year old son, who had been sold to a neighboring planter. When he heard men with dogs coming, he knew he would be treated like a runaway. He managed to hide, and days later contracted himself for a year to a boatman. Then one day, he was spotted, and the wrangling began between the boatman and the planter. That's when the case came to court. Father settled it by buying off both of them and bringing Sam home to us."

James told his friend about Callie's request. George readily agreed, saying, "I don't know her whole story, but I know that her children were sold away from her, and she nearly became violent. Somehow, she was brought here. It was about the time my mother was giving birth. When both she and my little baby sister died, I went into a very troubled state. Callie loved me back to sanity, much to Father's relief. She will always have a place here."

George breathed a deep sigh, and continued, "I have been so shallow most of my life. I'm just beginning to comprehend what a wonderful man my father was. He touched many lives, always promoting justice and compassion."

"He left quite a legacy in their hearts and ours," James said respectfully. "I'm afraid, though, that his example is not being followed by many. Maybe, somewhere, right now, there is a child growing up who will carry the torch for the rights of all mankind." The time had come. James said, "Shall we go into his study?"

"Yes. This will be the hardest part of coming home."

"It is as your father left it. It will take days for you to go through it all," James said as he opened the door. "On the desk is a letter of commendation and condolences from the governor."

He thought his friend would like to be alone, but he was asked to stay. "We have to talk. I have something important to tell you." James felt he was about to learn what had made George so preoccupied on the tour.

"My bride-to-be will be arriving next month," was the sudden announcement. He launched into a flurry of explanations and descriptions of their meeting as travellers in Venice.

James, recovered, grinned widely. "So you have found the one woman in all the world who is just for you. How wonderful! Congratulations!"

"Yes, thanks. But it will mean so many changes, it scares me."

"Life is full of changes. That's what makes it interesting," James declared.

"I'm especially grateful for the improvements you have made. Her parents did not want her to leave England and come to the 'wilderness.' I did some bragging about the estate to convince them that her life would be comfortable. Maybe, we should have married in England and traveled together. Her parents insisted that she needed more time for preparation. I know her father still had doubts. Actually, it was her mother who persuaded him that Elizabeth should make the decision herself. Elizabeth agreed to spend another month with them, thinking this would prove her firm resolve; but she told me to make all the arrangements for the wedding. I know she will come unless her father prevents her."

"Well, I've never been around a skittish bridegroom before, but I have a feeling that everything will work out fine. It always has." James tried to assuage his friend's anxiety.

"No, not always. I've seen something of the world now, and I've met couples that are cold and destructive to each other. I don't want that ever to happen to us. I only know that we love each other very much, and I want her to be happy."

"When you love each other so much, you will surely find ways to make each other happy. Isn't that the way it works?" James asked. Both young men keenly felt the lack of a role model of their missing parents.

"I suppose so." George was relieved to have expressed the concerns that had beset him on the long voyage. "Well, I must get busy and make those arrangements. You will be my best man, won't you, James?"

"Naturally. I'm flattered, but I don't know what that involves." James found this exciting.

"Neither do I, but I think the priest will be able to educate us on that. I must talk to Mr. Herndon, too. I want Elizabeth to stay with them the days before the wedding. I think she and Sarah will get along well . . . or is Sarah married?"

"No, she is still at home." James wondered if George had noticed the flush in his own face.

"With all the gifts her family has showered on her, she will be bringing quite a dowry. I suppose she will make some changes in the house," George opined.

"Of course, she will. Isn't that a woman's prerogative?"

"Yes, I guess it is. 'Life is full of changes.'"

It was already late afternoon when they thanked Callie for the meal, and got the wagon to get George's loads from the dock. "How are your muscles?" James asked. "It's been a long time since we chopped trees."

"My muscles are perfectly all right," George retorted. "Marble and granite slabs are not for weaklings, either."

Riding home together, George talked enthusiastically about his work. "There are so many buildings needing to be built here, that it boggles my imagination. This land will one day be dotted with architecture that came right from here," he said, tapping his forehead. "You'll see."

"I believe you," James affirmed.

It was a week before the wedding. Everything that could be arranged in advance had been done. Elizabeth would be arriving within the next two to six days. Sam had groomed the flower beds to perfection. No weeds were allowed in Bessie's garden. Martha and Callie had polished the house and its contents until it gleamed, and now, all the women were in a flurry of baking. George had not noticed his friend's pensiveness, and when the latter asked for a meeting, he expected more comradely banter, instead of the serious conversation that followed.

James began, "George, I really believe that you should put in writing your wishes about the use of your land, and also the provisions for Sam and Callie and the others. We've seen how unexpected events can complicate a man's affairs.

"Luke and Bessie will complete their indentures in another year. Martha can take over from Bessie, but that leaves no one to help in the house. Callie has managed it single-handedly these past years. However, there was no social activity during that time. That may change.

"Now, Charles says he would like to have his fiancee come. She works as a house-servant, and it would take a long time for her to save enough for her fare. She might be willing to come indentured to serve the future Mrs. Farland."

George had been absent-mindedly nodding assent. Now, he smiled and said dreamily, ". . . the future Mrs. Farland . . . I like the sound of it."

"Actually, I also came to talk about me," James told him. "First, I believe it is customary for the indentured servant to receive his contract marked 'completed' at the end of his service. Mine should be here in the study somewhere.

"Second, your father said he had set aside a stipend of ten shillings per month during the three years of my indenture here. He said it was available to me when I wanted it, but I had no use for it then, nor a place for safe-keeping. That would have been a sum of eighteen pounds for the thirty-six months.

"When I agreed to remain here and continue to manage the estate, he promised to pay four pounds per month plus sustenance. That was two years ago in June—twenty-five months—making one hundred pounds, plus the eighteen, a total of one hundred eighteen pounds. I don't know if the terms were ever written anywhere. We only shook hands on the agreement. I need to know where I stand."

George's consternation grew as his friend spoke. He covered his face with his hands briefly before speaking. "James, I haven't done my duty by you. I've simply taken you for granted . . . again. I apologize. Give me twenty-four hours to make amends."

"Thank you. That brings up another matter. As I wrote you, I knew nothing of your father's banking methods, and so I managed on a pay-as-you-go basis. No one here lacked any necessity, but neither was any money paid out for replenishing clothing and shoes, unless it was absolutely necessary. All estate expenses were paid in cash. All profits were deposited with Mr. Herndon's group of business and professional people who have some banking system among themselves. He seemed to be your father's most trusted friend. According to my books here, there should be a credit of three hundred twenty pounds," James explained, presenting the book with the page opened to the last accounting.

"James, you are a jewel. What would I ever do without you? Just don't ever leave me." When James did not answer, George exclaimed, "You *are* planning to leave, aren't you? Oh no, say it isn't so."

"At least, I'll leave the house for now. It will be better for all of us. I can stay on a while to help with the farm, but Charles is capable of taking over. Really, I don't know what to do with my life. I was going to ask you if I might live in the cabin we built until I make some kind of decision."

"Well, of course, you may; but that's rather primitive."

"It will give me time to think," James said ruefully.

George was as good as his word. A conference with the editor confirmed that there was, indeed, a sizable sum in his account, much of which had been added in the past three years. "You were very fortunate to have someone like James to look after things," Mr.

Herndon said as he explained the late judge's finances. George learned that fiscal responsibility now rested on his shoulders.

The next day, when they met in the study, George had the air of a business man. James received a statement of his own account which had been set up in his name to be drawn on only by him. One hundred eighteen pounds! James stared at it emotionally—his first bit of ownership.

"You will be interested in these other papers, also," George said, handing him two folded documents. One was his writ of indenture marked *Completed.* The other he read twice in astonishment.

"What! What is this? George, what have you done?"

"It is a well-deserved bonus, such as my father would have been pleased to give you. He had even discussed it with Mr. Herndon." It was a deed to the land on which the cabin stood and three hundred and twenty acres surrounding it, the surveying of which was to be started as soon as possible. "Hello, Neighbor," said George, extending his hand. James fought back tears as he took the outstretched hand and was soundly thumped on the back in brotherly fashion.

Elizabeth's arrival brought jubilation. George, who had been pacing the dock until the ship drew near enough to see her, now stood stock still, his whole being flooded with pleasure at seeing her again. She had come as promised. She was waving discreetly, smiling, impatient to be off the ship and in his arms.

James and Sam waited at the wagon. "Here comes the lady of the house," James said. If Sam felt any apprehension, he concealed it well and smiled broadly. James could see how his friend would have fallen in love with her. Her light brown hair and fair skin flushed with the elation of being in love, presented a beauty that charmed him instantly. Her easy cordiality made everyone comfortable in her presence.

They chatted amiably while George tore himself away long enough to direct the unloading of her luggage. "If you will choose what you need before the wedding, we can take that with us in the carriage, and the rest can go to the house in the wagon," George said, taking charge of the situation.

Charles had brought the carriage. Elizabeth's personal wardrobe had been placed in the back; George helped his fiancee into the carriage. Turning to James before mounting himself, he caught a nod and facial expression from James that meant, "She's all right. I'm impressed." George waved and grinned, and they were off to the Herndon house on Spruce Street.

Sarah had been thrilled to be asked to serve as maid of honor, even though she had not met the bride. They liked each other instantly. Mr. Herndon came home soon after their arrival, and tea was served—Elizabeth's first experience of domestic gentility in America. On the morrow, her trousseau would be unpacked and carefully pressed. She and Sarah would help each other, rolling their hair in strips of cloth, airing and fluffing her petticoats, choosing the flowers they would carry.

Marriage vows were to be spoken after the Sunday church service in front of all of the congregation that wished to remain. George and James, dressed in their new apparel, sat in the front pew while the ladies waited throughout the service in a side room. George wore a blue silk scarf knotted at the neck. It was a gift from Elizabeth. The worship service over, the two men approached the altar to await the bride and her maid of honor coming down the aisle. The men knew that they were looking at the two most desirable women on earth. James's heart skipped a beat at the sight of Sarah, strong and confident, attending Elizabeth, more slight and timid. Their hair, yesterday bound in strips of cloth, now hung in lovely ringlets; their faces, frankly alight with excitement, made them visions to behold. Lace caps added a fashionable, maidenly touch.

The vows completed, the wedding party and invited guests entered carriages and proceeded to the outskirts of town, where Mrs. Farland walked into her new home on the arm of her smiling husband. George had decided that out of respect for the Lord's Day (the only day the priest was available), and out of consideration for Elizabeth's unfamiliarity with her surroundings, the reception would be limited to twenty guests. There was to be no music and dancing, but instead, it would be an opportunity for her to meet close friends.

Sam greeted everyone at the door courteously, taking the men's hats and canes, and being sure that everyone had a seat. The ladies were offered fans. Soon the room was humming with greetings and conversation.

James heard conversation coming from the kitchen. He entered to hear Bessie and Martha assert that they did not want to serve "the likkers."

"I thought Jesus made wine for a wedding," Callie snorted, and picked up the tray, serving the bridal couple and guests with grace and dignity.

"It's only for a toast; after that, it's apple cider," James explained. They hardly heard him. Callie had surprised them with her reference to Scripture. They did not know, as James did, about her habits of Bible study and devotions.

"What's she like?" both of the women wanted to know from Callie.

"She's nice. She noticed me, even smiled," was Callie's reply.

Soon James was back to remind the women that it was time for the appetizers. Bessie quickly took the tray of smoked oysters on squares of toasted bread; Martha carried the tray of cheese squares with little wooden skewers in each. Now they would get a chance to see their new mistress.

Sarah had thoughtfully brought extra tableware and mugs to enable all guests to be served simultaneously. Her gentle hints to the men and her quiet conferences with Callie had done much to make the service go smoothly. Now she peeked into the kitchen. "Does anyone need any help in here?" she asked.

James stopped in the act of reaching for a tempting tidbit. "Oooh, Sarah, you look good enough to eat," he blurted, and then blushed at his effrontery.

"A rather big bite, wouldn't you say?" she quipped, and twirled to leave, with a backward glance that seemed to say, "I liked that."

"She needs a good man," commented Martha.

"I wonder why she hasn't married yet," said Bessie.

"Too independent," was Martha's diagnosis. James left the women to their observations and returned to his hosting duties.

Justice Henry was telling Elizabeth about days spent with Judge Farland. George was explaining his opinion about architecture for buildings being considered for the city to a group of townsmen. Other guests were strolling on the lawn. Time was passing pleasantly.

Then it was time for the three o'clock wedding banquet. Ham, roasted turkey, pickled tongue, venison sausage together with sweet potatoes, steaming green beans, savory squash, a large bowl of diced fresh fruit, breads, and three kinds of preserves filled a groaning sideboard. Elizabeth was amazed. She held James by the elbow and told him, "I wish that my parents could be here, but you are certainly filling their place as host. Thank you very much for all this."

James passed the compliment on to the others. "You ladies really did yourselves proud today." They beamed. It was the most delightful excitement of their lives.

At last it was over. James went to his own cabin. He had been packing his few personal belongings the day before the wedding, when George came in and insisted that he take all of the furniture that had been in the room. The cabin didn't look so bare now. He looked around at the repairs that would have to be made, but not tonight.

Now, he stretched out on the bed and let his mind wander. He had plans to make for his future. Why was it that visions of Sarah kept interfering with his thoughts? Her dark brown hair falling in soft curls around her shoulders, the color of her skin—that out-doors-y look, heightened by excitement, had been offset by the blue gown that seemed to draw out the blue of her eyes. Why had he not noticed before how clear and lovely her eyes were? Her straight-forward look had unsettled him several times during the evening. Unlike Martha and Bessie, he was glad she was unmarried. Sleep did not come readily that night, but it mattered not, for he would not be going to work at the big house tomorrow. He was in his own house now, and on his own land.

Tuesday was early enough to see what was going on at the master farm. George spotted him and called for him to come up on the veranda and sit. "We missed you yesterday, Neighbor," he said.

"Oh, really?" James answered, laughing. "Sunday was not much of a day of rest; so I took another one."

"Have you made any further plans for your future?"

"Not really. I don't know where to start. I might still try to go back to England and talk to former neighbors if I can find any." James was striving to focus his thoughts.

"Whatever you decide, the land will be waiting for you when you come back." George enjoyed feeling generous.

"That's a wonderful feeling. I can't thank you enough."

"Don't try. You've earned it," George said sincerely.

"Has Charles taken hold of the reins here? He's inclined to be a bit presumptuous."

"I think he feels ready to step in. He doesn't mind giving orders." Apparently, George was becoming more observant.

"If you decide to make him a paid manager in years to come, he should have less acreage. You want him to spend his time managing yours, not his." James was still concerned with equity among the workers. "Maybe I'll hang around for a few days and see that he understands the program."

"If you will be coming and going, you'll need a horse. Help yourself at the stable whenever you need one."

"Thanks, but I'm sure the horse would prefer your stable to being tied to a tree at the cabin."

"Well, the offer stands, if you need one."

By the time the month had ended, so had James's attention to the management of the Farland Estate. He had time to think now. His heart longed to visit Sarah, but his head reminded him that he had nothing but primitive surroundings to offer her. He could set himself to the task of improving the cabin and land, but she would still be entitled to know what his family connections were, and he longed to prove them. If he went back to England, at least he might find his baptism recorded there, but could he convince the rector of who he really was? He didn't want to spend the bulk of his savings on ship fare, and then return empty-handed and insolvent. "I've worked on a ship before," he reminded himself. "Maybe I could hire on for the voyage." He decided to broach the possibilities with the captain of the next ship to dock. He would go unshaven so as to look the part of a salty seaman.

IX

The Experiment Concluded

Memories flooded back as he passed the auction enclosure. He had been there before to find Luke and Bessie and the others; this was different. It was his own destiny he was thinking about now. A little over ten years ago, he had stood there the first time. He passed on by to wait at the dock. He would approach the captain after the indentured servants had filed off the ship.

He watched the immigrants curiously as they filed past him. There! His eyes locked on the third one from the end. The familiar something about the stranger that stirred a remembrance was confirmed by his intense gray eyes that could turn so quickly from smiling, to sullen, to hard as steel. It was no longer the captain of this ship he wanted to see now. James followed the other buyers into the enclosure. From the sales master he learned that the man whose appearance had caught his attention was sentenced to seven years of indentured servitude for the crime of theft. . . . the age: thirty-nine; the name: Thomas Nash; the price of his indentures: thirty pounds.

James was grateful that George had put his wages into an account. With a written note he was able to supply the amount for the purchase of his former tormentor.

They walked to the post where the horse was tied. James mounted and motioned Tom to follow on foot. After a short distance, he stopped. "It's quite a long walk. You'd better mount up behind me," he said, reaching a hand down to help Tom up. The act was not accomplished with grace. The ex-captain's sea legs needed reform. "Not used to horses, are you?"

"No, I'm a seaman myself," was the curt reply.

They rode on to the Farland stables. "We'll leave the horse here and walk the rest of the way, but I want to see the master first. Wait for me right here, Tom."

When he asked for George at the house, Callie informed him that the couple had gone to Williamsburg by shallop and would be back in two days. Nearly bursting with the news he had to tell, James emphasized to her that she was to tell her master that he needed urgently to speak to him. Then the two walked on.

Entering the cabin, James explained, "There's a lot of work to be done here. I've lived here only a short while. We'll fix it up." There was no response forthcoming. James kept his orders and explanations short. They ate a meal of cornbread left from yesterday and some of the cheese Martha had given him as a housewarming present.

James pointed to the small loft he had built for dry hay, which he kept in case he had a horse to feed for the night. "You'll sleep up there." The crude ladder made of narrow boards nailed across a corner of the wall, made it difficult to ascend or descend without a creaking noise. The space from the ladder over to the floor of the loft, which consisted of boards laid at a wider angle across the corner, made it difficult to access. I'm sure he's going to try to run away, but not without my knowledge, James told himself.

"What's in your bag?" he asked Tom, who answered by loosening the drawstring and emptying on the table the change of clothing issued at the prison, a comb, and a worn kerchief. James nodded, and Tom closed the bag. His sullen behavior seemed impenetrable.

"It's been my custom to read from the Good Book before bed. I'd like for you to listen and give heed," James said as he took his Bible from the top of the chest. He turned to Matthew, chapter 5, and read the beginning of the Sermon on the Mount. Looking up at intervals without raising his head, he noted Tom's furtive glances around the room.

Putting the book aside, James thought, he's too tired to try anything tonight. With no exercise in prison and none on board ship, and the long walk today, he'll sleep tonight. It's the next nights I'll have to watch him. James stretched out on his bed and pretended to be asleep until the reality of slumber overcame them both.

The next morning, Tom was put to work chopping down a young tree to be used for shoring up the loft, with the bark being used for reinforcing the roof. James busied himself in the cabin, observing through the open door that Tom stopped frequently to rest and flex his hands. That's the hardest work he's done in years, and he doesn't like it one bit, James surmised.

Without a word to Tom, James went into the woods to find a rabbit caught in a box trap that he had baited the day before. He had thought it might be his last meal on his land if he were hired on for the ship's crew. He skinned it and dressed it, then placed it to boil in the pot. Next, he scraped and stretched the skin and pegged it on a board. His life would be different now, more frugal.

The labor improved Tom's appetite but not his disposition. When James called him to come in for a bowl of rabbit stew, the meal was eaten in silence. After a rest James said, "Now that the tree is down, we need to lop off the branches." He noted Tom's annoyance and guessed that his muscles must be quite sore by this time.

Taking the axe, James quickly chopped off the top of the tree to a flat smooth surface after measuring with a piece of rope the length needed to reach from the floor of the cabin to the bottom of the loft. The two largest branches succumbed to his hefty axe blows in short order. Watching, Tom realized that his master's strength was much greater than his own.

When the axe was returned to Tom, he grudgingly completed the task of converting the felled tree to a smooth pole except for the stubs of smaller branches that James told him to leave shortened to serve as pegs for clothes. When put in place, the floor of the loft was stabilized by the pole and the forked top branches cut at a level to form braces.

The rabbit stew remaining was brought to a full boil again and left to sit as nearly sterilized as possible till the next day. It would again be boiled in the morning and then eaten in the afternoon. Bread, cheese, an apple, and cups of hot tea constituted the evening meal which was eaten in silence.

Again James opened the Bible and told Tom to sit and listen. He read Matthew 6: 1-15. The reading did not interest Tom a whit, for his eyes roved around the room, his head craning to study every feature of the cabin. "Wash the dishes in the pail of water outside the door. When you are finished you may go to bed whenever you like," was the last order of the day. Remembering the ache of his own uninitiated muscles after wood-cutting, James surmised that Tom wouldn't run tonight either.

Tom was not overjoyed to hear that more trees were to be cut down the next day, but he accepted the task more gracefully. By afternoon he was even cheerful, and after their meal, took the axe without being told. James, observing from the cabin, knew that this was the night the escape attempt would be made.

James had cooked several cups of cornmeal, and the two men ate a bowl of it seasoned with bits of salt pork, fried crisp in the iron skillet. There was enough left to fry for breakfast, so he patted it into a bowl to form a mold. There were salt pork drippings in an earthen bowl beside the fireplace that would be good for frying the sliced cornmeal mush in the morning.

Tom was in his bed early. When James retired, he kept himself awake by recalling the first time he had met Tom. Lying quite still, James considered the possibilities for the confrontation that was sure to come soon. Then, like a honey bee that has probed numerous blossoms before making a beeline to the hive, his thoughts honed-in on one acceptable solution. An unmasking of his identity and a resolution of the conflicts of the past was imminent.

It must have been about four a.m. when there was a thud on the floor that alerted his senses to full acuity. Tom had not used the squeaky rungs, but had lowered himself as far as possible and dropped to the floor. The door opened with scarcely a sound, and he was gone.

In a few moments, James too went out the door, carrying the rope he had used the day before. The morning was cool, the sky partly cloudy with a bright moon peeking in and out of the clouds. He reckoned that Tom had gone down the trail by which they had arrived at the cabin three days ago. A good thing we used the hunting trail leading from the stables, rather than the short cut George and I took when we walked out here, thought James as he started down the short cut.

Tom soon lost the thrill of adventure as he followed the dimly lit trail, thinking how different it looked at night. A rabbit scurrying ahead of him startled him; a turkey hen sitting on her nest clucked a warning when he nearly stumbled on her. The owls with their eerie "Whooo" created momentary panic. Such were not the sounds of the sea he had known. He knew he had nearly reached the stables when he stepped into the clearing.

Somehow he would mount a horse and ride to another seaport, and hire on for work that would take him far from here. He had stepped into the stable when he felt a loop of rope slip over his head and shoulders, pinning his arms to his side as the noose tightened at his waist. He heard his master's voice say calmly, "We'll go back now." And they did.

Dawn was beginning to break as they neared the cabin, but the clouds had thickened and now a light rain was falling. Upon entering the cabin, James led his servant to a spot near the hearth, dropping the end of the rope he had held. He squatted and brushed away the ashes until he found a glowing ember to which he added small bits of wood until there was a lively little flame. By adding larger sticks, he would soon have a good fire.

Loosening the noose and letting it drop around Tom's feet, James ordered, "Take off your shirt." Tom may have for a moment expected that the fire would be used to brand him as a runaway, but he was relieved to see that James was removing his shirt as well. "Hang it across those two pegs up there at the side of the fireplace to dry," he was told, as James did the same with his shirt at the other side.

Turning around to look at James who was again tending the fire, Tom saw in its glow something he had almost forgotten. At the top of his master's scarred back, between the shoulders were the scars from branding "T \." It couldn't be! How could it be? He bent down to get a closer look as his mind raced to remember the circumstances that had caused them—the boy on the dock, the hostility and frustration he had released, the boy's resistance, the meat storage room, the glowing rod he had used to make those scars. That same deceived indentured servant was now his master, with good reason for meting out immediate punishment as well as long-term retribution.

James rose, faced Tom, and asked, "Have you seen something fas-cin-a-ting, Captain Thomas Nash?" James had seen fear in the face of a rabbit he had trapped for food before it was quickly dispatched, but that was not comparable to the growing dread in Tom's expression as the full realization of his situation seeped into his consciousness.

The men looked at each other in silence. Then James spoke sternly, "The first thing I want to know is how many other boys you used in your experiment, and where you have taken them."

"None. No others. You were the only one. I ran a legal shipping service, but I was so very angry that day. . . ." His voice trailed off.

"Good! Then this is just between you and me. Where is your ship?" James demanded.

"Confiscated. The customs officer found rum from the West Indies under the floor boards and charged me with smuggling. I tried to tell them it was bound for France, but they didn't believe me. They said it was subject to tariff anyway." The need to answer gave momentary relief from a deeper problem.

"But what did you steal?" James questioned.

"A silver snuff box. I only did it to make trouble for the surly waiter. I didn't even keep it. I had given it to a beggar." Tom was trying to justify his motive, if not his action, but James was not impressed.

"You were angry about a waiter when you met me before." Tom's eyes lowered. James pressed on, "Not the same one . . . after ten years?"

"I had been back as a guest of an owner who wanted to buy my ship for trade in the islands. This time I was alone, and he refused to serve me. I thought he would be blamed for the loss of the silver. He was in charge of offering it to the guests. He was a snob! After my arrest, my ship was searched."

"I see. Because you had to get even, you stole; and because of that you lost your ship. Such foolish resentment!" James shook his head, then brought the interrogation sharply into focus with, "It's very important to you to even old scores, to take revenge, isn't it? Do you think I should do the same?"

"Oh God!" Tom gasped, pounding his fist against the wall in helpless consternation. He could offer no defense.

"I doubt that was a prayer. From the way you behaved when I read from the Bible, I have to believe that you have no fear of God nor respect for your fellow man. And yet, it's that Book that teaches me that I should forgive you." James spoke evenly, quietly, but Tom seemed too befuddled to comprehend.

As he turned back to the hearth and placed the skillet over the flame, James continued, "God forgives me my sin when I repent and trust that His Son, Jesus Christ, has paid for them with his own suffering and death. He rose again to give us new life. Without Him, I could never forgive you, nor would I even want to, but now . . ."

Tom heard the words but understood little of their meaning. He saw James invert the bowl of cornmeal mush and shake its contents out on a plate to slice it. Turning again to the skillet, he reached for the bowl of pork drippings, poured some into the skillet, and with his finger wiped the drops hanging on the edge of the bowl into the skillet.

All the while, James continued speaking, ". . . now, I believe that we must put the past behind us. You can turn a new leaf, build a new life, be an honorable man, and have all the *real* respect you always wanted." Turning to get the slices of mush, he saw the knife had disappeared.

Tom was holding it in his hand, staring at it uncertainly. "Oh, Tom, don't be foolish. I'm offering you a chance for a better life. Why would you want to spoil it?" James asked. Tom said nothing.

"Give me the knife, Tom." James tried to sound confident but soothing.

Suddenly Tom snapped into action. "No, no," he shouted. "Stand back. You had your fun toying with me, but I'm not as easily fooled as you were. I won't be humiliated any more, and you'll never see me hang either."

James had been slowly inching forward. Now, seeing Tom's desperation, he knew that talking would accomplish nothing. He lunged forward pinning Tom against the wall, both hands holding Tom's wrists. "Drop the knife, Tom," James said calmly.

He was easily overpowering Tom, but Tom had learned tricks on the streets of Liverpool that he had never forgotten. Instead of resisting the grip on his wrist, he went limp. He had felt the trace of grease on James's hand, and when the latter eased his hold, he wrenched free from the grasp.

In an instant, James lost his footing because of the release of resistance, and fell across Tom's chest. The knife plunged into James's side and remained there as Tom released the handle. He shared the look of disbelief he saw in James's face as the latter sagged to the floor.

"No," Tom screamed. "No, no . . . not you." Then he was on his knees beside his fallen master, reaching for the knife to remove it.

James had let out a cry of pain, but now spoke in short gasps between breaths which caused him to wince with each movement of the rib cage. "Wait . . . let blood clot . . . you have time . . . repent and live . . . not me . . . Father, in heav—" The words faded away. The blood loss and the pain caused shock to take over the wounded body and mercifully produced unconsciousness.

To Tom's credit it must be said that he had not planned this outcome. In the past months, his perception of himself as a self-made man had undergone disintegration. He had lost control of the destiny he thought he held in his own hands. His self-esteem had been annihilated. His master's unexpected generosity had unnerved and confused him. Now the inert body labeled him a murderer. In panic, he ran from the cabin and down the trail.

George and Elizabeth had returned from Williamsburg. It was most enjoyable for her to see the fine homes and well-kept gardens of that more genteel city. She had met people who were cultured and prominent in their fields, as George delightedly introduced her to friends of his father. On their ride home, they had discussed the role they would play in bringing advancements to Richmond. "It's good to be home," Elizabeth had said, and George was relieved to know that her interests lay at Farland Estates.

Sam and Callie welcomed them warmly, and for those two faithful servants it seemed that happy times were returning. Callie remembered the urgent message left by James two days ago. "First thing in the morning I'll ride over there," was George's response. Then he had a joyous thought. "Sam, you used to go with my father when he hunted. Early tomorrow morning, come with me through the woods and show me where you went. We'll stop at the cabin as we ride."

Sam beamed and responded with a dignified, "Very good, Master." Sam had taken to addressing him now without adding "Master George," acknowledging him now as the sole and total proprietor of his father's possessions.

The morning dew was still heavy, but the rain had ceased when Sam and George rode down the hunting trail. George's sense of loss in remembering that he had never ridden here with his father was interrupted by Sam's exclamations as he pointed out places where a deer had been brought down, a turkey spotted, or a fox observed streaking toward his lair.

Suddenly, they were confronted by a disheveled man, running panic-stricken headlong down the trail. When he saw them, he gasped, "Please, come and help. My master is badly wounded."

The pleasure jaunt was now shattered. George presumed that having a man to help clear land was the information James had urgently wanted to share. It had to be his friend who was wounded.

"Get on behind Sam," he shouted to the man as he spurred his own mount and raced away toward the cabin.

Horrified at the sight of James lying motionless with a large clot of blood protruding from a wound in his naked side, he stood transfixed. Tom came in behind him and said in amazement, "He came to. When I left, the knife was still in him. He told me not to take it out, but wait for the blood to clot, then he passed out. He must have come to and pulled the knife out himself." With his fingers on the artery in James's neck, he reported excitedly, "He is still alive."

George roused to action. "Sam, go to the pharmacy and ask Doc Hannibal to come right away. Take my horse with you so that you can both ride back as fast as possible."

On his knees beside his unconscious friend, he struggled to decide what to do. "I'm afraid to move him for fear of more bleeding. Let's cover him, except for the wound. It is a good thing he wasn't wearing a shirt. There are no bits of cloth in the wound." Turning to Tom, he asked, "Why are you both without shirts on such a cool morning?"

"We got them wet in the early rain."

"The rain stopped two hours ago. Surely you weren't out working in the dark," George went on relentlessly.

Resigned to being discovered for his deeds, Tom answered, "No, I had run away and he brought me back. While he was starting breakfast and had his back turned, I took the knife, intending to take my own life, but he saw me and tried to take it away."

"He is strong as a lion. You could not have overpowered him."

"No. I tricked him." Tom added the details of their fight. He leaned against the wall, weak with fatigue and remorse.

Too sorrowful for wrath, George told the dispirited figure before him, "This is the kindest man in the world, and you wanted to run away from him. That was very foolish."

Doc Hannibal's credentials derived chiefly from working with physicians on various battlefields. Fallen soldiers with life-threatening wounds were carried to makeshift hospitals and cared for as humanely as possible until their last breaths. Little attention was given to curing or healing ministrations except for amputations of mangled limbs. If recovery occurred, it was an act of God, not man.

He inspected the wound, the knife, noted James's pallor, and shook his head solemnly. "There is nothing that can be done to save him. He has two days at the most. He has a pulse and the bleeding has slowed, but that knife punctured a lung if angled upward, or the intestine if downward. If 'twas in the lung, his breathing will get more and more shallow. If 'twas in the intestine, he'll have bowel contents running loose in the abdomen. He'll run a high fever, be delirious, and beg for water. You must not give him any, though, or he'll bloat something terrible, and that's a horrible way to go. I'm sorry." Even the air seemed heavy with grief as the verdict shattered hope.

"Is it all right to move him to the bed?" George asked.

"It doesn't matter one way or the other."

"Thank you for coming. I'll send your fee in a few days."

"There's no hurry, Mr. Farland. You're your father's son."

Sam stood with tears running down his wrinkled cheeks. "Sam will ride with you and bring the horse back," George said. Doc nodded and left. His composure appeared unruffled, befitting a veteran of many scenes of bedside suffering.

Such was not the case inside the cabin. Tom, recognizing that he was now in deeper trouble than ever before, gave that only a passing thought. Something else stirred more deeply inside him: This man should not, *must* not die. Despite humiliation and deprivation, this man was loved and honored by both high and low. Tom's own egotism and resentment had degraded him to acts of crime and cruelty. He knew that he alone was to blame for his disgrace.

George sank into a chair and faced his wounded companion. "Oh, James, why?" he moaned amidst tears. "Your life was just starting to flourish after those years of hardship. You changed my life, dear friend. We'll miss you so." The mourning continued until, remembering that he was not alone, he bestirred himself to action.

"Fetch water. Be sure that the pot is thoroughly clean, and then heat the water. Clean up this table. Put on a shirt." Tom was glad to be doing something. It was when he heard George say, "Gather up your things. You'll be coming with me," that he obeyed with reluctance.

When Sam returned, he was asked to remain with James. George and Tom rode back to the estate. "Charles, this is Tom. He belongs to Mr. James, but he'll work here for now. Keep him busy and out of mischief."

"Yes, sir, Mr. Farland. You may be sure that I will." Noting George's sad countenance, he refrained from further comment and led Tom away to the sorghum field where harvesting had begun.

George related the morning's events to Elizabeth while he assembled towels, sheets, a blanket, and toilet articles. "I want to remember him looking clean and comfortable. He has the look of peace as he lies unconscious." Elizabeth had no words adequate to comfort, but touched his shoulder in loving understanding.

Sam and George stripped off the bloody trousers, washed the still body, and lifted it on the bed covered with clean white sheets. The bulk of the clot had slithered off, and a dressing covered the wound secured by a bandage wrapped around the body.

"Sam, I need you to stay with him today. Callie has sent you this lunch. I'll be back before sundown and spend the night." Sam nodded. George returned to seek solace in the amenities of his home and the condolences of his wife. In the back of his mind were thoughts of a burial plot and a funeral service that needed to be arranged.

When Mr. Farland returned from James's cabin the next morning, the field hands had not yet left for the fields. Tom, risking the manager's displeasure, approached the horse and rider. He took the reins from him but refrained from asking about James's condition.

Seething with indignation, George ignored the servant who stood there with unasked questions written all over him. After a few steps, he thought better of it, and said tersely, "He lives, but is getting restless, starting to beg for water," and with that walked away to get some rest. Tonight, George thought, is when the end will come. I must be there and hold him in my arms.

That night was balmy with a bright moon shedding an air of cheer and tranquillity across the land. But inside the cabin there was no peace. George had come having steeled himself to share his friend's parting moment, but he was not prepared for the sight and sound before him. Delirious, James pleaded almost constantly for water, reaching weakly toward his friend, although it did not seem that the glazed eyes recognized him.

George could bear it no longer. James was not even aware of his presence and was too weak to hurt himself by falling off the bed. He stepped from the cabin, breathed the clean woodsy air, and let his mind roll back to the time when he and James first began building the cabin that had led to his own pursuit of architecture. He walked over to the spot where they had felled young trees. The stumps were still there. If things had been different, James would be planting this area in a crop next spring. George recalled their proud moments of achievement, their arguments, their enthusiastic hard work. "Here is where we grew from boyhood into manhood," he murmured, "and here was supposed to be his big opportunity." Enough of this. He had come to be with James at the end. He must return to the cabin.

His first impression at the door was that the pleading and babbling had ceased. Was the end already past? A dark form kneeling at the bedside moved, and he saw that it was Tom holding a cup of water to James's lips, trying to restrain him from gulping it too quickly. Momentarily stunned, George shouted, "What do you think you are doing?"

"I think Doc Hannibal is mistaken. The knife did not enter the lungs; there were no air bubbles. And it did not enter the intestine; the bleeding was clean, not mixed with digested food." As he was being roughly pushed away, Tom continued, "He is dying from loss of blood and thirst, but he could still live if he has liquids."

George looked down at James, now calm and resting. Still he challenged Tom. "Doc Hannibal served an apprenticeship with Dr. William Cabell, the best know physician in Goochland County, in the whole colony in fact. And you presume to know more than he does?"

Tom's confidence was unsettling even while it brought a glimmer of hope. "I only know this," he said. "In the West Indies, I once saw a pirate hung from the bowsprit of a ship docked next to mine. He was drawn and quartered before my eyes. The executioner cut open his abdomen, and his bowels were removed while he still lived. Blood was everywhere, but the lungs and heart remained in place. There must be a strong partition dividing them from the belly. That is where the knife entered, I believe. It may have nicked the liver, but that could heal, if only we do not let him die of thirst."

For a long time George said nothing, then grimly declared, "If he lives, he will deal with you; if he dies, I will."

"I know," said Tom. "If he dies, I hang for murder. If he lives, I hang for kidnapping."

"Kidnapping?" George asked astounded.

"You didn't know? Those are my initials I branded on his back ten years ago after I kidnapped him off the dock and sold him into slavery," was Tom's disheartened answer.

Speechless, George stared at the two men whom providence had brought together a second time. Further questions would have to wait until another time. He was more concerned now with wondering how Tom's action would affect the outcome.

James was again asking for water. Tom picked up the cup but looked at George, waiting for a signal. George shrugged, resigned to letting events take their course. Tom let his master drink freely this time, and James soon slept again.

When Sam came to relieve the bedside watch, it was Tom who said, "He can have water now whenever he asks for it." Since Mr. Farland said nothing, Sam agreed.

The men rode back in silence. Upon reaching the stables, they saw Charles, annoyed and agitated, asking everyone if they had seen Tom. "Keep him busy and keep an eye on him. Don't let him anywhere near my family," George said as they dismounted. He heard Tom getting a tongue lashing from the manager. He'll be lucky if he doesn't get more than that before this is over, George thought as he entered the house.

That evening when he left for the cabin, he carried a jug of Callie's rich beef broth wrapped in a blanket, and led the spare horse for Sam's return.

"He seems to be more comfortable," George observed with great relief. He sat watching his friend's regular breathing. Could it really be true that he would live to take his place as a free "builder of the nation?" That had been their self-proclaimed title while they were building the cabin and dreaming of castles in the sky.

The next time James stirred, he drank eagerly of the nutritious broth. He opened his eyes briefly, and George thought he saw recognition and even a faint smile there before the eyes closed again, and stupor overcame them.

About two hours later George was standing in the open doorway looking skyward when he heard "Is there any more of that broth?' George was actually laughing as he held the cup to James's lips. "Yes, yes, you may have all the broth you like."

"Thanks. Nobody makes broth like Callie." James slept again.

It was early morning. George had fallen asleep with his head resting on the table, his shoulders covered by the blanket. James lay awake on his bed until he saw George stir. "What happened?" he asked.

"What's happened is that you've just come back from the dead," George exulted. They were still talking when Sam arrived and joined the rejoicing, ready to assume the day watch.

Charles forbade Tom's approaching Mr. Farland when the latter rode up, but spotting him at the stable door, George gave a hand signal that cheered Tom immensely throughout the day of cutting sorghum. Sorghum, he had learned, was not a prime crop in Virginia, but from it came the sweet ingredient that made other foods more enjoyable. "I must plant some for my master," he promised, "to take away the bitterness I gave him."

That evening Sam returned before George left to relieve him. "Mr. James told me to leave and to buy these supplies at the market before coming back. He said that you did not need to spend the night, that he is nearly well. He also asked me to bring Tom tomorrow."

"He has been sleeping for most of three days. He'll be restless tonight and try to do too much. I had better stay with him. Oh, Sam, do you remember the pallets we used to take to the cabin when we camped out there years ago? I'll take them, and we'll probably talk half the night like we used to."

They did, indeed, spend many hours talking, about past incidents as well as the most recent one. "You're not going to keep Tom here, are you . . . just the two of you?" George asked.

"I don't know. I guess it will depend on his attitude."

"Or his acting. He deceived you with his acting before."

"We'll see. Please keep his past confidential, George. I don't want it to be public knowledge, and I'm not sure how to handle this. People will be uncomfortable around him if they think he is dangerous."

"I haven't even told Elizabeth. I was so upset about his giving you water, that was all I talked about." They slept at last and it was bright daylight when they awoke.

Tom had slept little that night. Since being told that he was to face his master, he had been turning over in his mind the right things to say, planning the ways in which he now wanted to serve. Yes, he would turn over a new leaf, as James had offered.

Sam went to the market early, and by mid-morning had purchased the supplies requested. He and Tom rode off together. At last Tom had the opportunity to ask questions about his master's welfare.

George met them outside the cabin. "He's waiting for you. Remember, he tires easily, so don't upset him," he told Tom.

Sam's answers, optimistic as they were, had not prepared Tom for the sight of seeing James sitting on the side of the bed, pale and weak, but alert and stern.

"Oh, sir, it's good to see you sitting up and getting stronger," Tom exclaimed.

"Good morning, Tom. I asked you to come so that I could tell you personally what is about to happen. As you know, Mr. Farland has spent a great deal of his time nursing me back to health. But now the time has come that I should be on my own again. I need someone here whom I can trust." Tom was smiling and nodding eagerly. "Therefore," James continued, "I've asked Mr. Farland to take you, and to bring back someone to stay here who has no reason for wishing to see me dead."

Tom had stopped smiling. "No. No, don't do that," he shouted impulsively in great agitation.

"What did you say?" asked James sharply.

"I . . . I'm sorry. I mean, please, don't send me away," Tom stammered, flustered by a development he had not anticipated.

"Surely you don't expect me to place myself in your hands a third time when the last two times nearly cost me my life, do you?"

"Oh, Master, I don't deserve that you should believe me, but—God is my witness—the knife was never intended for you. It was my life—my worthless life that I wanted to end, not yours." He was trying desperately to organize his plea, but it was all coming apart.

James pondered. "Even if I could believe you, there are other facts to face. You have been a captain for years, accustomed to giving orders, not taking them. In my weakened condition it would be you who would be in charge again, and there would be nothing I could do about it."

"No. Please. For days I've been planning how I would serve you, not for just seven years, but for the rest of my life. I owe you that. I know how much I've wronged you, and I accept any punishment you decide; only, please, don't send me away."

So far there had been no self-righteous attempt at justification, but James wondered if this were honest contrition, or mere fear of the unknown. He said, "You misunderstand me. I'm not sending you away to be arrested, only to be sold. I leave vengeance to the Lord. You can carry out all your lofty resolutions any place where you will be among strangers, and not have a one-to-one daily confrontation."

"But there is so much I need to learn from you. No one ever cared enough to talk to me as you did. Even when it seemed that you were dying, you told me I still had time to change."

"You do, and you will have ample opportunity to prove that you are changed, but I can't have you here imposing your will and vexing me with your insubordination."

Tom searched desperately for words. "Master, you said you would forgive my crimes against you. That was more than I could have hoped for, but I beg you to forgive me again for still pleading with you. I swear that I'll cause you no more vexation. You will have my instant obedience for any order you give me."

James was thinking, "Yes, if it happens to please you. Well, let's put this to a test." Aloud, he said in a voice that was seemingly hard with finality, "Really! I have given you only one order today—to go with Mr. Farland. I hardly call this instant obedience."

Totally dejected, after a long pause, Tom answered in a hushed voice, "I will go then," and turned to go.

James was satisfied and was about to call him back, but Tom had turned at the door, remembering something about their last parting. He said, "I am going, but there is something I must do first." In a swift motion, he knelt and kissed his master's feet.

George was at the door. "Tom, get up. Help me get him back to bed. Take his feet and raise them without twisting his body."

Tom saw James's face white as a sheet, drained of blood and weaving in a near faint. The change of position soon revived him. Tom was told to wait outside by the horses. George stayed with James, and they talked a short while before he came out.

"You left your bag inside. You'll be needing it," Mr. Farland said with a motion of his head toward the cabin.

Silent and hopeless, Tom re-entered the cabin. He had lost the anchor he had clung to for purpose in his life these past days. He picked up the bag, but then he heard hoofbeats of horses galloping away. He stared at the disappearing riders, turned to James and stuttered, "They are . . . l-leaving . . . going away."

"Right. It's just you and me again," James answered. "I needed to find out what you would do with an order you didn't like," was the brief explanation. "Now, how about some breakfast? I seem to be hungry all the time lately."

Tom seemed about to collapse with the effort to control himself. James spoke briskly, "Sam left the supplies on the bench outside. They need to be brought in . . . when you're ready." That private moment would help Tom regain his composure.

They had finished breakfast when James said, "Thanks for the water . . . the other night when I was dying."

Tom flushed with pleasure, but was still burdened. "It must have seemed that I was begging to stay only to escape the flogging Charles promised me for leaving that night. But I want you to know that I am really and truly sorry for what I did to you . . . and so ashamed." He hid his face in his hands.

Touched, James answered, "I believe you. Now you should believe that you are really and truly forgiven. The Bible says, 'The blood of Jesus Christ cleanses us from all sins.' You and I both need that. You see, I have a Master, too; so we'll both kneel before God, but no more to each other." There still might be snags in their relationship, but now they could talk them out.

Later that day, James showed Tom how to bait a box trap for rabbit with an apple core balanced on a slab of wood connected to a trip cord. When an animal entered to take the bait, the released cord would drop the door of the box shut, leaving the animal unhurt inside. "If we can't make this work, we'll be eating beans and salt pork all winter," he said.

James still needed long periods of rest each day. He lay looking about the cabin planning improvements that needed to be made. He fretted about the light-headedness he felt when he stood or sat up for long periods, but he was glad to be strong enough to take care of his personal needs. "I won't be needing this 'old salt' beard anymore," he said as he gathered his shaving articles and proceeded to remove the ten days growth of whiskers. The heat of late August had made them most uncomfortable.

He was glad to be clean-shaven for another reason that afternoon. Trying to keep cool while resting on his bed, he had begun to doze when Tom came to announce, "Someone is coming up the path." It was probably George, he thought, coming to make sure that he was following orders to spend most of his time in bed for at least another week.

"It's a lady," exclaimed Tom.

Wide awake now, James ordered, "Quick, throw me my shirt. Clear those cups off the table and wipe up that spilled tea. Toss my shoes over here. Hang those clothes up on pegs. Now, go out to greet her and help her with her horse."

Tom gathered that this was a special lady. However, help she did not need. Before he could get out a greeting, she had dismounted, draped the reins over a sapling, and was striding toward the cabin swinging a wicker basket covered with a bright cloth. Tom had time only to say, "Good afternoon, madam," to which she sang out, "Good afternoon. My father sends this basket to Mr. James. Is it all right if I go in to see him?"

A nod was the only answer Tom could give before she swept past him and headed for the door. There, she paused as though her bravado had left her, but only momentarily.

When she entered, James had managed to reach the chair by the table and seat himself, so he was in a position to rise gallantly and welcome her. More demure now, she extended her hand, expressed her concern for his health and brought greetings from her father, all quite properly. He felt those lovely eyes on him, searching the gauntness of his frame. "I brought . . . my father sends you this basket to cheer you in your recovery and to extend his very best wishes." Pulling back the cover, she revealed cheese, fried chicken, a small ham wrapped in cheesecloth, a dozen eggs, fresh apples, two loaves of bread, and an earthen jar of apple butter.

James grinned with delight. "If that doesn't speed my recovery, nothing will. You are an angel to be so thoughtful and kind." Seeing her blush, he went along with her subterfuge. "I must thank your father personally when I see him."

"Oh, I will give him your thanks. You concentrate on regaining your strength."

"How did you know that I had been wounded?" James asked.

"George asked my father to have a prayer for you in church last Sunday. Many people remembered you from the judge's funeral and the wedding. They all wish you well."

Increasingly, the cabin seemed crude and inappropriate to James as he looked at her sitting on the only other chair he owned, with her lacy sleeve touching the unfinished table. The silence was becoming embarrassing until she looked about her and said brightly, "So this is the house that James and George built."

"We thought we had built a castle by the time we had finished it," James replied with an expansive gesture.

"It must have been quite an undertaking for two sixteen-year-old boys." She spoke as one who understood the labor involved.

"We resolved many differences of opinion and learned a lot about tolerance before it was done," James said laughing, and began recalling some of their difficulties. The conversation was lively and jovial. It was easy to converse with her.

"And now it is yours entirely, I understand," Sarah stated.

"Yes. George, as well as his father, were very generous to me. These past days I've been trying to decide what to do. I had thought of adding another room, but we might just put up an entirely new cabin—if George will come and tell me what I'm doing wrong." He was relishing every moment with Sarah, but it was time for her to leave. Their manners were quite proper, their emotions less defined by rules of etiquette.

Sarah's visit was tremendously healing for James. He would do all in his power now to make a home to which he would bring her some day. He had to admit that the day might be well into the future, but the secret ambition was his to hold and cherish.

He would purchase a cow, chickens, and some sheep. They would need a shelter for the winter. That meant cutting down more trees for the logs, thereby clearing more land for crops. Still more trees would be cut to provide logs for the bungalow he envisioned as a proper home for Sarah. He chafed at having to wait for further healing.

Tom, returning to the cabin, reported that he had lost the rabbit as he reached into the trap, but James said, "That's good. We won't be needing any for a week at least," anticipating the feast from the basket.

September brought the start of rains and some relief from the heat. James found the ground soft enough to yield to some cultivation. Weeds pulled out easily and were piled at the side of the clearing. On his first visit back to the big house, Bessie gave him a few seeds of mustard and spinach. "You might get a few carrots and small beets before frost, if you are lucky," she said as she wrapped seeds in four separate scraps of paper.

He had been invited to tea by Elizabeth and George who still cautioned him about getting back to farming too soon. "We hear that you had a lovely visitor a few days ago," they said, smiling at each other knowingly. Sarah had stopped there to ask directions to his cabin.

"Yes, Mr. Herndon sent us a very ample basket of food. It was very kind of Sarah to bring it," he replied. Things were still a bit too tenuous between himself and Sarah for him to feel comfortable discussing any plans. Sitting there in their handsome parlor, he thought of his home in stark contrast. Was he presuming too much? Friendship was one thing, but would his lack of apparent heritage discredit him as a lifetime partner for a woman as wonderful as Sarah? Still nagging his self-confidence was the recollection of the instance of the Tornsons' distrust even after he had served them well; the derision of the Russells even when he had proved himself more intelligent than they; even George's steadfast generosity was sometimes a reminder that he had been a pauper. The sweet anxiety of his yearning spurred him on. He would pursue his dream.

"Oh, by the way," he said as he was leaving. "If you have an axe that is not in use, could I borrow it until I can get to town and buy one?"

"Sure," George agreed. "Just be sure that it's Tom who swings it." He knew that James already had one axe on the premises, and a second one meant that his friend felt fit to resume normal activity. A word of caution was in order.

X

The Perils of Authority

James found that he was not as ready for hard labor as he had hoped, but each day he attempted more. He and Tom worked well together. With Tom being left-handed, they could coordinate the axe blows alternating from both sides as they felled one tree after another. The stumps, left from when he and George had worked there, were now weathered enough to be removable. A fall garden flourished at that site. Tom knew nothing of his master's secret urgency but enjoyed being involved in the project.

They started to build the shed for livestock that James would buy. Fashioning it like the one he had seen at the Tornsons, they notched and fitted the logs together to make a fair-sized room for shelter in extreme weather, plus a one-walled extension on the north side that would be adequate for most of the year. Experiencing the satisfaction of his first construction, Tom exclaimed, "This is fine enough for humans. It's luxury for animals."

"Aye, and we'll have to rest a while now. These spasms in my back are getting worse. I can't get a strong swing anymore. I guess you've noticed that you have been doing most of the work." James told him. Tom understood why James had groaned while working, and why he had become downright irritable sometimes. The bungalow that he had hoped to have completed by spring would likely not even be started by then. Tom pleaded with him to rest thoroughly until the pain subsided, and James had to agree that it was necessary.

Glumly, he lay staring around the room. His eyes fell on the two pallets George had brought on his last overnight stay—relics from when they first slept in the cabin. They hadn't even finished the building, but they couldn't wait to spend the nights there, sleeping on the rough floor, catching glimpses of moonlight through the unsealed cracks. Tom had said, "This is fine enough for humans," speaking about the animal shelter. That's about the way the cabin was once. Yes, it was good enough. . . .

"Tom. Tom come here. Listen to this. We have about ten logs lying outside, right? You can split them in halves, several of them a day, right? Then, they could be fitted to build a floor, something like this one, in the shelter?" Tom was nodding assent as rapidly as the questions were being asked. "You could build a sunken fireplace leaving a space in the wood floor and mounding it up with clay leaving an air vent to the outside. With the shorter logs, you could build a bed, right?"

"Yes, but why? What are we aiming at?"

"Indentures are selling very cheaply now because of so many ships coming in before winter, so this is the best time to get ourselves some help, right?"

Tom was glad that his muscles had developed into firm, efficient machines as he split the logs, wrestled them into place, and fitted them together for the shelter floor. James did the lighter work of filling in the cracks between the logs with clay. A mound of clay formed a shelf halfway around the fireplace. For a temporary home, it's not bad, he thought.

James had assembled all the rabbit skins that had been curing for the past two months. Now, he fastened them together with sinew as the Indians did and surveyed his blanket with satisfaction. Tom had fashioned a low bed and stool.

It was Friday morning. The weather was cold and blustery, and James's back hurt more again, just when he thought he had noticed some improvement. Neither walking nor riding horseback would be wise to undertake, and yet this was the day when indentures would be sold in town.

"Tom," he said, "I don't want to wait another week or two. I want you to go to the auction and try to find a boy of about fifteen years or a single man who can help us. Take this note to Mr. Herndon's office and ask the clerk to give you twenty pounds from my account. If you can't find the right person, then use some of the money to buy several laying hens at the farmer's market. We can at least perk up our diet. If we absolutely have to, we can wait for the next ship, so bring the rest of the money home."

Tom was surprised to be given such an assignment, but agreed without questioning.

"When you get to the Farland house, tell George that you are on an errand for me, and that I'd appreciate his lending you a horse. That way you'll get to town earlier. It really means a lot to me to get this work done this winter."

That afternoon James took the rabbit-skin blanket and the two straw pallets out to the shed. One pallet served as a mattress, the other folded in thirds, formed a pillow. With the blanket placed over the bed, it looked quite cozy. He started a fire in the fire basin and set a candle ready to be lit on the clay shelf. I don't have to apologize for this, he told himself. It's better than the sacks I slept on in that print shop. Besides, the lad will likely be homesick. We can help him. It will be good for Tom to have someone to work with and teach. The three of us can really turn this land into production. By spring the bungalow will be ready. Tom and the lad will have the cabin, and this shed will have the floor boards removed and be turned into an animal shed.

The prospect of seeing his dream realized was exciting. He hoped that Tom would be able to find the right person for the job today.

He prepared the stew for supper and began to await their return. He wondered what Sarah was doing today. She and their cook, Jenny, would be working with the fall fruits and garden produce. Jess, their gardener and houseman, would be raking leaves, mulching their flower beds, and caring for his master's personal effects. They were not landowners, but Mr. Herndon's work as newspaper editor and financial manager provided the household with influence, prestige, and a good, if not generous income. Their two servants were loyal and dependable, and the household ran smoothly. Looking around, James told himself that the changes he was making would make his place suitable for his bride.

He paced the floor and the yard, growing ever more anxious, since it was getting dark, and Tom had not returned. At last he saw two figures approaching. He seems quite small, James thought, but then, I was only twelve when I began felling trees. He stirred the stew and waited for them to enter.

Stepping over to the door as he heard their voices, he stared at the smaller figure with surprise turning to disappointment, then to anger. Tom said, "The Farlands were not at home, and Charles wouldn't let me borrow a horse. I walked both ways and we are late. Sir, this is Becky Sloane." Tom's confidence faded away as he saw his master's mounting displeasure.

"Take her to the shelter immediately," was James's brusque order. Tom made as if to continue an explanation, but when James shouted, "Immediately," he said no more, and the two walked to the shed where he lit the candle for her.

"What is the matter? He seemed so angry," she asked in worried tones.

"You are not quite what he expected," Tom said hesitantly.

"Well, I hope the mistress will like me."

"Oh, there's no mistress. Now don't worry. I'm sure he'll come to you later." With that, he was gone. She had been eager and talkative on their walk, telling him her story and expressing her hopes for her new life. He didn't see her countenance pale, and her eyes become troubled. He had to talk to James now.

At the cabin, James handed him a bowl of stew and square of cornbread. "Give her this," he said tersely. Tom complied and quickly returned to find that his own supper awaited him on the table. "Aren't you eating?" asked Tom.

"Not now," was the reply. While Tom ate, James moved about the cabin restlessly, alternately stepping outside and returning. Tom had barely finished eating, when James sat down facing him. Making an effort to maintain his self-control, he said, "Now, let's have an explanation."

Cheerfully, Tom began, "I was late getting to the auction, though I don't know if that would have made any difference. The only indentures available were for couples, a carpenter, and one who claimed to be a mason. I had started to leave, when Becky was brought forward, and then I saw what the commotion was about across from me. There were two young men with an older man, their father I suppose. They had been making rude remarks to her, sort of smacking their lips as they told their father, 'We want that purty little thing right there.' They were all quite drunk. Others were shaking their heads in sympathy, but no one was bidding except

Mrs. O'Neal from the inn. Then she stopped, too, when the price went up. The girl was so scared, and shaking so much she could hardly stand. The auctioneer had called for a close on the bid, and the boys were whooping and jeering. The bid was nineteen pounds, ten shillings. I looked at your twenty pounds a second and shouted a bid just before the bidding closed. Just then she fell in a faint. The auctioneer asked me to carry her away. We sat at the side of the street for a while until she recovered, and then we walked away. The rowdy fellows came by and mocked us, saying how lucky they were not to have put their money on a sick weakling. I tried asking Mrs. O'Neal to take her, even for less than I paid, but she said she had no use for a sick child. Master, she is not a child, and she is not sick," Tom declared, "only scared out of her wits. She walked home without once faltering, and she is happy to be here. She'll do well."

James's face had softened a little as Tom related the story, but now his voice was heavy with sorrow. "But I can't be happy about this. Tom, did it ever occur to you that I had a very special reason for wanting this land cleared quickly to bring in an income? The bungalow was to be built by spring so that I could ask the woman I love to be my wife—so that I would have something to offer her. Now, all those plans have come to a crashing halt."

"Oh, Master I didn't know." Tom was annoyed with his denseness in not guessing. The lady with the wicker basket of goodies . . . of course, she was the one. She had smiled at them Sunday when they were in church.

Sorrow was turning to bitterness as James replied sarcastically, "I didn't think I had to get your permission. But that's not the worst of it. My bride-to-be is the daughter of a prominent man in the church, the lay reader whom you know. Her ideals are at least as high as mine. What do you suppose she will think when she hears that I sent you to withdraw money from my account in her father's office to buy a young woman to live here with the two of us? But you wouldn't understand that."

James continued speaking agitatedly. "There will be plenty of gossip, but her opinion is the only one I'm really worried about, and I know her. It's the end of everything between us. I don't know what kind of standards you have lived by, but for me marriage is a life-long union with no outside alliances before or during. I'm sure those are her standards, too, as the church teaches. How am I going to explain this to her?"

Tom was distressed. "I am so sorry. I thought I was doing what you would have done if you had been there. I was even pleased with myself for being compassionate."

"Not compassionate with me." Anger was seeping into every word and frustrating thought. Control was rapidly slipping away as James paced the room.

At last, Tom spoke hopefully, "If I married her, would that make it all right?"

James's control snapped. "So that's it!" he shouted. "You really do have the advantage, don't you? It's just as I feared. Now you'll have what you wanted all along. The mighty Captain Nash with a woman in every port! How you must have felt deprived!" He pounded the table with his fist. "Of course, you couldn't wait."

"No," shouted Tom. "I meant it only for your protection."

"The smooth-talking Captain Nash," James stormed on. "He'll guide me around his ship. He'll obey every order without question. He'll ruin my life as long as I let him."

"Please, tell me what I can do," Tom pleaded.

"I'll tell you what *I* can do," yelled James. "At first light, I can take you both into town and hand you over to the sales master to keep until the next auction. Then I'll start all over again. Understand this," he spoke through tight lips, his face near Tom's, "you will not deceive, betray, or manipulate me ever again." He realized that he had reached a breaking point, and struggled to control himself. "I'm going to take a walk. When I come back, stay out of my sight." Then he stalked out of the cabin.

Tom sat confounded. He had never seen James in such rage. What would he tell Becky? It had seemed so right to rescue her. If he had left the auction sooner this would not have happened. He had disobeyed; but what would have happened to Becky? He cleaned his bowl and ascended to the loft, his heart aching.

As James walked, the cold air tempered his anger. Already, he acknowledged that his chronic nagging pain and the strength of his desire had amplified his disappointment and his reaction to it. It supplied no answers, however. He walked a ways into the woods and turned to look at his home, only a tiny rustic cabin and a shed intended for animals. He remembered that in the shed was a girl who must be perplexed by her reception and worried about her future. He would have to tell her that she would have to go back. He owed her that much of an explanation.

Slowly he approached the shed. A faint light could be seen through a crevice of the roof beams. His knock brought no response, either the first time or the second. The door yielded to his touch as the latchstring still hung outside. She rose from her stool when he entered. She had removed her coat and hat, and he saw in the flickering candle light that she was very pale under her mass of auburn hair. "Why didn't you answer? I thought you might be on the floor in a faint . . . again."

She made no reply but stood with her hands clasped in front of her.

"You have let your fire go nearly out, and it's going to be very cold tonight. There is firewood right outside the door. You must try to keep an ember glowing throughout the night, or you'll be sorry in the morning." He stepped outside to get two chunks of wood. As he did so, he thought, I came here to deliver a hard message, and here I am, waiting on her.

Rather gruffly, he showed her how to bank the fire to maintain its heat, when he noticed her bowl of stew. "You haven't eaten anything," he exclaimed.

"I wasn't hungry," she said in a very low voice.

"When is the last time you ate?"

"Yesterday."

"Then you absolutely must eat. Here, I'll set the bowl in these hot ashes to warm it a bit."

She remained motionless. What's her problem? he asked himself. Aloud, he asked, "Does the thought of rabbit stew disagree with you? Here in the woods, rabbits are equal to chickens. They are actually better than chickens. Their hides made excellent blankets," pointing to her bed.

She seemed to give a start. He thought for a moment, then said, "Look, if it bothers you to sleep under animal skin, just turn it over and sleep under the fur side, and you'll be more comfortable."

Going to the bed he took the blanket and turned it over. With the disturbance, the folded pillow moved a bit. A glint of steel caught his eye. He stooped down and reached under the pillow, coming out with a sharp scissors in his hand. He stared at it a moment before the significance of his find became clear to him. Looking at her sternly, he said, "I suppose if you had gone home with those three men, there would be some dead people by now."

She came alive at the accusation. "I would rather die fighting than be a lumber camp whore," she protested.

"And now you were expecting me . . . " James was comprehending.

"I was expecting that there would be a mistress. Tom didn't tell me there were only the two of you. Then when I asked why you were so angry, he said that I wasn't what you expected but that you would come to me later." The slight figure faced him half in defiance, half in apprehension.

His mind tried to grasp the dread she must have had of this day and, even worse, of this night. "You need have no fear. Tom and I are both honorable men." Trying to calm her with practicality he asked, "Do you sew?" as he handed the scissors back to her.

"Yes." She was visibly relieved. "I helped my parents in the tailor shop in Manchester."

"Are you ready to eat now? I'm going to stay here until you do." There was a flicker of a smile as she accepted the food and began nibbling on the cornbread. "Made from maize meal—a new food of the New World," he explained. "You'll like it once you get used to it."

She had started on the stew and was soon eating eagerly as she sat on the rough seat by the fire. Even though she was short in stature and fine-boned, her features appeared mature in the firelight. "How old are you?" he asked.

"Nineteen."

"Honest?" He hadn't taken the time to read her papers.

"Honest. People have always thought me to be younger than I am," she asserted.

He sat on the edge of the bed. "Do your parents know that you are over here?"

"My parents are dead." She had stopped eating. "The shop was part of our home. When the fire broke out in the shop, my father ran to get my mother. Together they tried to save some of the materials and equipment. They died in the heavy black smoke. I had gone to the market. When I came back everything was gone."

"Had you no relatives?"

"Only my mother's brother who lives in Liverpool. He came, and after the funeral, took me to live with them. His wife hated me. Her twenty-year-old retarded son liked me too much. They said we should get married and take care of each other." She shook her head. "When they kept insisting, I left them a note, went to the docks, and signed for my indentures."

James blinked. Her concise account belied the days of grief and dread that had surrounded her. "How long ago did all this happen?"

"Seven months ago that my parents died; seven weeks ago that I left Liverpool." Her voice was steady, showing no sadness. She had been forced to make practical decisions to survive. Her seeming hardness covered her vulnerability and would not allow her to express her grief. James understood.

"Well, finish your supper and get a good night's sleep. We'll see you in the morning. Good night," he said rising to leave.

She curtsied. "Good night," she said pertly. Then as he was going through the door, came a "Thank you," with a tiny quiver in her voice.

He smiled and left. Now what am I going to do? he asked himself as he returned to the cabin. I never should have let her tell me her story. No, that's not right either.

He knew one thing he must do at once. "Tom, are you awake?" he called, and immediately heard Tom's "Yes, sir."

"Come down, please."

As Tom faced James uncertainly, it was plain that sleep had been far from his mind. "Tom, I was wrong. You were right. If I had been there, I probably would have done the same thing. I'm sorry for my harsh words and my selfish anger," James told him.

"You had good reason to be angry. I am sorry for all the trouble I've caused. Is there any solution? What can be done?"

"Well, for tonight we'll sleep on it. In the morning we'll see how God wants us to work this out." He spoke with assurance but also with remorse. "You know, Tom, what really scares me is that, down in my heart, I didn't actually believe that you acted deliberately to disobey, but in my frustration I wanted to lash out and hurt you. So I used words that would cause the most pain. It's so easy to misuse authority. I'm truly sorry."

"I'm the last person in the world who could fault you for that. Believe me, I do understand what frustration does to a person," Tom said fervently, protesting James's need to apologize.

"Another thing, before our struggle, we used to read Scripture. I felt that it guided my thoughts, words, and actions, but since I got on that building campaign, I have neglected that. I told myself that I had read through the New Testament twice in the last three years and knew what they contain. I know now that one needs to stay close to the Word, or the devil snatches it away. Stay with me a few minutes while I read."

Opening the Bible, he said, "Let's see, we had been reading in Matthew, chapter six, through verse fifteen. Do you remember this? 'For if ye forgive men their trespasses, your heavenly Father will also forgive you; but, if ye forgive not men their trespasses, neither will your Father forgive your trespasses.' I especially wanted you to hear that, but I doubt that you were listening at the time. Maybe now we've both learned to listen. Let's read on to the end of the chapter."

As James read, he began to smile. Looking up, he saw that Tom was listening, hearing for the first time, and comprehending that there was wisdom in that ancient book. James silently prayed that Tom might also accept the salvation offered there. The chapter ended with, "Take, therefore, no thought for the morrow; for the morrow shall take thought for the things of itself. Sufficient unto the day is the evil thereof."

Tom lay on his bed of hay. He had thought that the Bible was for weaklings and people who used it for the power and influence it could bring them. He had considered all those who preached it to be hypocrites. His master certainly was no weakling nor hypocrite. It was more than mere honorableness that made him different. When James had talked about forgiveness, a yearning to know more had stirred within him.

At early dawn when he awakened, Tom found James already out of the house and leaning against a stump. "Have you found any answers?" asked Tom.

James shook his head. "Only that we can't throw her to the wolves. She doesn't even realize the problem this causes."

After a long silence, Tom spoke. "If I understand correctly, the damage to your reputation has already been done by her being here last night . . . unless . . . "

"Go ahead. Unless what?"

"Master," he said sincerely, "when I spoke of a marriage last night, I meant that it would be in name only. I had no intention of making her my wife except in a legal document—a marriage of convenience. Isn't that what many marriages are anyway? After her indentures are served, she could leave in the same condition she arrived and move to another colony even, if she wishes. In the meantime, she would be safe, your reputation would be clear, and I would be . . . behave."

James laughed in spite of the occasion. "You would behave, huh?"

"It wouldn't be as difficult as you might think. My old sea captain was a woman hater, said they were nothing but trouble, and kept me away from temptations of that nature. Later, there was Lizzie, only Lizzie. She worked in an inn on the waterfront and was somewhat retarded. The sailors harassed her with teasing and insulting propositions. One day I told them that she was my woman, and they should leave her alone or meet me in the alley. She was warm, loving, and grateful. We were close and loyal. She waited faithfully for my returns. Then one time she was gone. A co-worker told me that she had died while I was in the West Indies for a long time. I was never interested in any one else."

"Why Tom! You've been hiding sterling qualities under that tough mask of yours. I wouldn't have figured you to be a rescuer of damsels in distress." He was glad to know that Tom likely did not harbor the diseases of many promiscuous seafarers.

Tom hastily returned to the problem at hand. "We'll build the bungalow for you and Mrs. Bankstone. Becky will have the cabin. I'll move to the loft over the shed. I'll be the coziest of all with all that animal heat in there," he smirked, remembering a load of livestock he had once shipped.

"You'll be yearning for a fresh sea breeze by morning," said James.

"That only guarantees that we will have the cleanest animal shelter in Virginia," Tom replied, undaunted.

"You make it sound simple, but I fear there would be hidden burdens. What if you would change your mind about 'in name only?' Becky is an attractive woman."

Tom brushed it aside as being of no probability, but then stated, "If it comes to that, I would come to you, as her father, and ask your permission and then propose to her as if the marriage were just beginning. There, is that proper enough?"

James shrugged. "I have no other solution."

"May I go and explain it to her?"

"Yes, but then I want to talk to her also. I have to be sure she understands and agrees without constraint."

"Would I be too persuasive?" Tom asked in pretended shock.

"Yes, you would," was the rueful answer.

With breakfast over and the matter settled, James urged them to leave at once for the church. "If the priest is to conduct services at Hopewell tomorrow, he'll be leaving by noon. Here is a note explaining that Becky arrived only yesterday and a civil ceremony is requested. That eliminates all the complicated vows that would be required in a church ceremony. I believe that all that would be asked is your mutual consent. You should be able to sign the papers and receive your certificate right away.

"I don't know what the customary fee is for such a ceremony, but here are fifteen shillings which is all I have on hand. If that is not enough, tell him that I have been unable to get to town and will make up the sum next week. Now get going. The earlier you get there, the more honorable you appear."

As they started down the path, he called after them, "The church is only half as far away as the docks. I'll expect you back earlier today." He prayed that they had read God's will correctly. With no other answer forthcoming, they had taken the only one available.

He wished that he could do something festive to celebrate the start of the new relationship. He was tired of the drab fare they ate and the dull look of the cabin. Even the trees, shedding their leaves, seemed disconsolate. He felt himself floundering insecurely.

The tiresome rabbit stew needed to be boiled again lest it spoil before evening. While replenishing the fire, he remembered that Bessie had said he'd be lucky to get some carrots and beets before the first hard frost. A trip to the garden reminded him that he had not picked mustard greens in the past week. Sure enough, there were young carrots and beets large enough for several worthwhile bites each. He had the making of a more interesting meal. He cleaned the carrots to add to the bubbling stew. He washed the greens and boiled them with a strip of salt pork. The beets he would boil in their skins and peel later to nest on a bed of chopped greens. He had to keep washing out his two pots to be able to cook the rice also, which he found among the remnant of items Sam had brought two months ago. He picked the last of the lantanas and centered them on the table.

By two o'clock he was impatient for Tom and Becky's return. Suddenly they were at the door, looking very pleased with themselves. "Come and eat while you tell me how everything went," he urged.

"First we have to take care of these," they said gleefully, holding out three hens they had hidden behind their backs.

Was it really only yesterday that James had been so severely disappointed? Now he was looking at a pair of smiling servants who were exceedingly eager to please him. He had no idea what might come of this, but surely it couldn't be all bad with so much good will present. He felt a light-heartedness as if a benevolent authority had assured him that he was not to worry; everything would be all right. They were waiting for his response. He gave a playful scowl and asked in feigned disapproval, "Where did you steal those?"

Tom grinned. "We didn't steal them. Father Maddox said the fee was seven shillings. He had to leave quickly after the ceremony. As we were walking away, his housekeeper tried to get his attention. She needed money for the market, but he was out of earshot. Becky asked her what the price of a hen would be. She said, 'About a shilling, six pence, but that's not what I need to buy. I have too many now, plus a basket of eggs that I don't need with him gone so much.'"

Becky took up the narrative. "I told her we would buy three hens if they were good layers. When I gave her five shillings, she said, 'I really need all of this for marketing.' When I asked her to give us the change in eggs, she decided that she would also sell some of the eggs in town, so we were all happy."

"Even Father Maddox will be happy when he returns and finds food on his table," Tom added.

"This is wonderful," James exclaimed, adding in playful dismay, "but what happens if on a given day, only one of the hens lays an egg?"

"Then it's yours," they chorused.

"Unless," Becky interjected, "I get it first to make noodles."

"You make noodles?" the men exulted.

"Sure, and many other things. We must be sure, though, to save all the meat drippings." (What bliss having her take charge of the domestic details!) Becky was saying, "Here are your remaining three shillings and the dozen eggs," as she took them from her bag which only yesterday had held her very sharp scissors and a few personal items.

"I found a surprise, too," James said. "Here are the first of our winter vegetables. They'll grow even more before the first hard frost."

"The best place to keep them would be in a corner of my room since this cabin will be too warm from the cooking."

The men were smiling, thinking that eating would become a restorative pleasure from now on. James asked a blessing and gave thanks for the way God had brought them together and guided their little community. Silently, he added a plea for forgiveness if their actions had not been in accordance with God's will, and help for his own future that had gotten so unexpectedly complicated.

Mr. Herndon would be conducting the service this Sunday morning. James, with the other two, had arrived early and presented a request for a prayer of blessing on the marriage vows spoken yesterday by Thomas Nash and Becky Sloane upon her arrival from England. After the church service, James asked Tom and Becky to go on without him. He would remain in town for a while.

While they were walking home, Tom stopped and listened. "Where is that singing coming from?" They followed the sound and soon found themselves at the edge of a group gathered in an open area.

"It's a revival meeting," Becky stated.

"What's a revival?" Tom wanted to know.

"It's when a visiting preacher comes and preaches to people from all different churches. People who haven't been in any church for years, or never, will come rather than attend their own church. But if they are truly revived in their faith, they usually become active in a regular church when the visiting preacher moves on. There was a Rev. Whitefield in England that many people came to hear and he traveled all over."

"Did your family go to hear him?"

"No, but we did hear Rev. Wesley last year several times. I don't remember too much of what he said, but my parents were impressed and talked about it often. They were good people."

The preacher's voice thundered out over his audience, "Don't think that being a 'good person' is going to save you. If you are trusting in your own self-righteousness to help you stand before Almighty God, you are deceiving yourself, my friend. The only way a sinner can stand before a holy God is if Jesus covers him with his own perfect righteousness and says, 'Your sins are forgiven.' Without that, your righteousness (pointing) and yours, and yours, is nothing but a filthy rag in God's sight. That's what the Bible says."

"He sounds just like Rev. Wesley," Becky whispered. "He could really stir up his listeners."

"I wish Father Maddox would stir us up a bit more," said Tom.

The sermon had ended, followed by a prayer, and groups of people came forward to speak to the preacher who had promised to return in one month. Tom and Becky strolled leisurely home.

XI

Lives Joined

James had been walking, too, but not so complacently. After leaving the church, he had headed in a different direction where he would not likely meet anyone who knew him. As he walked, he was meditating, hoping, preparing what he would say . . . and then it was time to do it. He turned toward the Herndon house.

There he saw Jenny carrying out dishwater and pouring it into the flower beds. She was willing to take his message to Sarah, asking her to meet him by the apple trees. He supposed that this was not how it was done properly, but how could he talk to her father without knowing beyond all doubt her feeling for him?

Then he saw her coming with that energetic stride of hers, her dark hair fluttering in the wind. She had changed from her Sunday dress to a simple figured frock with white ruffled trim, and she wore a dark blue sweater.

Though friendly, their meeting was awkward, both of them uncertain. They began with small talk. Sarah remarked, "Whew! It has really warmed up since this morning. Will you help me out of this sweater?"

She turned her back to him, and he pulled the garment down off her shoulders. With her hair drawn to one side and hanging down over her bosom, she was a vision. Before either of them knew how it happened, he kissed the back of her luscious neck, and she whirled and slapped his face. They stared at each other. Her hand raised to her lips, she looked into his eyes filled with pain, shame, and chagrin.

"I . . . I'm s-sorry. I had no right," he stammered and turned and ran from her. He heard her call his name. She would want to talk, to be reasonable, to be kind; but that would hurt too much. He didn't stop. If only he could run to the end of the world and jump off! He had misread all their interaction. There was nothing for him where she was concerned. His thoughts ran faster than his legs.

It was not until he heard her scream, "James, please help me. My foot . . ." that he turned to see her lying on the grass.

He ran back, and kneeling beside her, straightened the leg, asking, "Where does it hurt? Is it in the ankle or in the foot?"

She had gotten very still. Now, she sat up and held him firmly by the arm. "Neither one. I had to get you back. If you hadn't come, I would have been heartbroken." A little embarrassed now, she continued, "Oh James, I used to dream of how it would be if you ever came to call. You would dash up on your horse and jump off. I'd run out of the house to you, and you would take me in your arms."

This was almost more than he could stand. He slipped from his knees to sit facing her as she went on, "When, after all that scheming, you kissed the back of my neck, something in me snapped. I was surprised and acted from reflex." She was blushing. "When I first started to school, the boy who sat behind me used to tickle me there every day with the feather of his quill pen until I slapped him hard every time he did it. James, I am so sorry. I didn't mean it."

James could only stare. Was this really happening? He shook his head and blinked as if the fantasy might end, but it didn't. "I, ah, was coming to ask your father's permission to court you," he explained, "but first I wanted to see you—to give me courage, I guess."

She smiled the most enchanting smile and looked deep into his eyes. "I came prepared to give you courage. The sweater removal trick was supposed to do just that. Only, you were supposed to take me by the shoulders and turn me around, and wrap your arms around me. I'd look up into your face, and you would bend down and . . ." Her eyes were warm and tender.

"Like this?" he asked, as he raised her chin and touched his lips to hers. The new sensation was breathtaking, ecstatic, stirring emotions that cried for fulfillment. They both understood that this was the beginning of their future together.

"I can't believe that I told you all this, but it seemed so natural to say it," she said, leaning her head against his shoulder.

"I hope that we can always be honest with each other. It's wonderful to understand our own feelings and to be able to trust each other with them." It was a dreamy moment, but James remembered that he had come to clear away all doubt. "Sarah, does it bother you that you know nothing about my family—that I seem to be a homeless drifter?"

"You are neither homeless nor a drifter. Besides, it's *you,* not your family that I love."

"Maybe we should let your father in on this," he suggested.

"He'll be reading on the veranda, waiting for his tea. Now is a good time."

He found Mr. Herndon just as she had said. Sarah's father greeted him warmly. "Come, sit down, and have a cup of tea."

"Perhaps, I should state my business first. You see, sir, I have come to ask your permission to court your daughter." There! He had said it!

Countless young lovers, as well as their parents, know that such a question takes longer to answer than any. Actually, it wasn't all that long before the man said, "My daughter is of an age to speak for herself."

"But we would appreciate your approval."

"You have it. Now, let's have our tea." James felt himself relaxing. The hard part was over, though this was not yet a marriage proposal.

"Sarah, you had better come join us," Mr. Herndon called.

Sarah had taken the tray from Jenny and was already coming. The rapture in her flushed face spoke volumes to her father who had begun to worry about the single state of his daughter. As she served them, he noted the affection that passed between them. Aloud, he blurted, "So this is why you refused to see Father Maddox. Well, pour me another cup of tea, and then you two had better run along."

They strolled down the walk, arm in arm, James had never been so happy. "I feel sorry for Father Maddox. Did you break his heart?"

"There wasn't much heart to break," she asserted. "He thought it would be 'a good idea' for us to marry. It's not like we were going to be devastated without each other . . . not like us."

Able to speak freely now, they shared their hopes and goals. James told her of the bungalow, the garden, the livestock, the increased acres under cultivation. "Oh Sarah, I want to make a splendid home for you, for us; but it will be simple at the beginning."

"And I don't want to be left out of the development. I'm a pretty hardy soul, but still I was happy to hear that you had another woman at your place. It would be lonely with two men to take care of and no help for all the domestic duties. You fellows be good to her until I can get out there to help. Elizabeth told me that Charles's fiancee is coming soon, too."

James felt a little dizzy. If he had asked for a sign, this was surely it. Knowing that he must soon leave, James held her at arm's length and asked, "Sarah, at this point, would you say that we are engaged to be married?"

A look of mischief crossed her face as she said coyly, "Why do you ask? Have I said anything to make you think I love you?"

They laughed together deliciously. Then James got serious and said, "Now let me ask properly." Kneeling on one knee, he said, "Sarah, I love you with all my heart. Will you be my wife?"

She was serious, too. "Yes, my beloved, I will be honored."

Delightful as his embrace was, she couldn't resist a playful, bold, "When?" as he released her. "See? I've quit scheming."

"We will have to save that for next time. My heart is already overflowing with happiness. If it bursts, I couldn't come to see you next Sunday."

It was Tom and Becky's turn to be concerned when James had not returned at dusk. When he did come, the light in his face was not to be concealed. "We need to get that bungalow built, and get ready for a wedding in the spring." They congratulated him with whoops of joy. Now he would have much to tell George and Elizabeth.

The weeks of late autumn and winter were needed for each of the persons involved to work through their feeling of anticipation. James longed for his father to be there for his wedding day, but consoled himself with the thought that he might be a father himself before many years. Sarah struggled with feelings of immaturity as she faced the new role of wife, and eventually, she hoped, motherhood. She had questions she could not ask her father, fears she remembered since her own mother's death. Elizabeth's friendship meant more to her as the weeks passed. The women had long conversations over their sewing.

Sewing was not Sarah's forte, but once she discovered Becky's proficiency in that art, she gratefully accepted her help and advice. Even so, her hope chest was scanty, but her many friends would add to it. Most of them had been married for several years already.

Mr. Herndon, influential, respected, outwardly a pillar of strength, struggled with the loneliness that loomed ahead. He had at times felt responsible for his daughter's tomboyish behavior, even while he was proud of her strength and independence. She could shoot as well as he, could ride better, and often came up with good ideas for publishing the newspaper.

The days flew by. James measured them in weeks, since each Sunday he would see Sarah, often spending the afternoon. George teased him, saying that love had even cured his back spasms since he was now able to work long hours again. It was understood that each Sunday morning James, Tom, and Becky would leave in time to reach the church early enough to get the seat near the back. James wanted to sit next to the aisle where he could watch his sweetheart coming up the aisle after the service.

Two people who were seldom, if ever, in church met them while they walked one Sunday morning. Two young men on horseback came into view around a curve and immediately reined their mounts to a stop. Becky tried not to show fright as they drew near. Tom, too, recognized them as the two who had urged their father to buy Becky at the auction several weeks ago. James recognized them as the Russell brothers who had given him so much grief in the preparatory school. "Don't bother to answer them. Just keep walking," said James.

"She looks to be in pretty good shape now," said Horace. "She must like being a slut for these two indentured servants."

"She coulda been a special woman at Dad's camp, livin' with free men. They'd give her nice clothes and jewels," Bruce jeered, "but she'd rather live with these two losers."

When they moved their horses closer, James told them evenly, "Neither of you can even stand up by yourself alone. Unless you protect each other, you lose all your nerve."

"You better take that back," Horace threatened. "This horse can stomp you into the dirt."

"Of course. Without your horses you wouldn't dare to harass two peaceable men and a lady. Your father has tanned your hides so many times that you are mean as curs, but you really have no courage. Why don't you split up? One of you sign on a ship and go to sea; the other, go help Col. Washington fight the French and Indians. Then we'll see if you're men, or just mean." James knew that any sign of weakness would only encourage them. Tom was restraining himself with difficulty.

Just then Mr. Russell came around the curve driving a team with a wagon full of supplies. He yelled, "Get along now and quit makin' trouble, you worthless idiots. She's bought fair and square, so leave them alone." The boys turned away just in time to avoid the snap of the long whip that lashed at them.

As our trio walked on, James commented, "I've tangled with those two before. I'm glad you're not with them."

Walter Herndon was getting reports on how the building of the bungalow was progressing. Sarah had added a few ideas of her own during the planning stage, but now she spent more time on her trousseau. "James is working so hard to build a little house for you, and we have a big house here that will be nearly empty if you leave it," her father reminded her.

She saw his sense of loss, but said firmly and tenderly, "I will come to visit you at least once a week, I promise. I cherish this dear house and will do so always. But after the wedding, I will go with James to his. That's how it has to be." He knew it to be true, but he would be lonely without her.

Later, Sarah came to James with news. "I just heard that Father Maddox is marrying the Widow Morris from Hopewell. She inherited the plantation from her late husband. He will be leaving Richmond as soon as he can be replaced." Letting that soak in, she continued, "You felt sorry for him. Now his wife will bring him a bigger dowry than I ever could have. All I will have as inheritance is a house and, eventually, Father's business."

"What does any of this have to do with us?" James asked, puzzled.

"Father has hinted that we could live with him. He will be so lonely."

James asked guardedly, "What do you want to do?"

"I've already told him that we are going to live at your house. But then, I got to thinking that you also will be an heir—part of the family—and I should ask about your wishes, too. If I was selfish, I'm sorry."

Relieved, he put his arm around her. "I like the answer you gave him. It's important to me to be able to develop this place and feel that at last I have a home. The only thing more important is your happiness. I'm sure he'll feel alone. Let's plan to visit him regularly, and also have him visit us in our home. That's all part of being a family, right?" She was pleased that the two men most dear to her would be considerate of each other.

One day in February, James and Sarah visited George and Elizabeth with a special request. "We hope to set our wedding date for April 15. Will you two be our attendants?"

"So it has finally come to this. Of course, I'll be your best man. Who else knows you well enough to keep you in line?" Then, remembering, he asked, "How about you, dear? Will you be up to a walk down the aisle by April? Let's see, that's about seven weeks from now."

"Oh, I'll be there. I hope you don't mind if I bring the baby along." At the announcement, James soundly congratulated them and the women hugged each other.

"May I come tomorrow and spend the day with you?" Sarah asked.

"Please do. We have so much to talk about."

The bungalow was nearly finished. Real glass window panes and planed floorboards coated with linseed oil and rubbed smooth, enhanced the ambience. James had ordered several pieces of furniture that would not be duplicated by what Sarah would bring with her. Flower beds built at each side of the front step were planted with bulbs that were already peeking new growth through.

Becky's homemaking ideas had included the purchase of a handsome cock. The hens were beginning to brood. In a month there would be baby chicks. A pregnant goat kept the weeds neatly nibbled as far as her tether would allow. The well-fertilized garden thrived.

The men had cleared enough land for small plantings of wheat, corn, and sorghum. They would still cut more trees before the hot weather came. The logs would dry during the summer. On any suitable day the thudding of the axes could be heard.

XII

Lives Rejoined

The men were unaware of the figure that stood watching them from the edge of the clearing. "Whoa, it's rest time," panted James and sat down on a stump. The man moved closer until they looked up at him. "James Bankstone, Jr?" he inquired in a voice rife with feeling.

"Yes." James rose, and the two stared at each other for a long moment, James struggling to remember.

The other spoke again. "I am James Bankstone, Sr."

In a flash it was clear. "Yes, Father," James shouted. Speechless, they embraced, looked at each other, and embraced again, incapable of an intelligible sentence.

Tom was transfixed as well, but with different emotions. He heard James say, "Tom, tell Becky to fix us her best meal. There will be no more tree cutting today. Father, this is Tom, my right-hand man. You probably met Becky who told you where we were working." Tom left the two talking animatedly.

The colleague at Oxford had finally been able to deliver the letter James had written five years ago. The father had returned from India only a few days before, and had set sail for America at his first opportunity. For both of them to recount all their experiences would take the rest of their lifetimes.

At the cabin, Tom watched the two men approach, still talking excitedly. How would the arrival of the father affect their lives? He tried to keep busy tidying the cabin and helping Becky prepare the meal as he coped with his anxiety.

James was glad that Becky had insisted on buying more tableware and cooking equipment. The table was quite presentable, though rustic, when he and his father sat down to eat. They had hardly begun when Sam, beaming, arrived with a note and a bottle of wine from George and Elizabeth. They regretted being gone when Dr. Bankstone arrived and were most eager to meet him. They offered him lodging at their house if he wished. In any case, they would be expecting them both tomorrow for a day-long visit and dinner.

"What do you say, Father? Do you want to sleep in comfort or rough it tonight?"

"I want to sleep where you sleep tonight. Tomorrow morning I need to go to the shipping office and pick up my luggage. I could stay at their place after that."

As James wrote a note in reply, he reckoned that his father would not find the accommodations of the cabin too primitive after the experiences he had related during the past hour.

His father had spent four years in India, just as the Oxford colleague had written. Before returning, he had decided to follow up on information of plants with healing and health maintaining properties that were to be found across the Himalayas. A guide had taken him through a mountain pass to the unexplored land of Tibet.

Immediately north of the mountains, he had found a sub-tropical wonderland of plants. The one he most wanted to find turned out to be a kind of foxglove, only slightly different from the ones in England. Older people with heart difficulties chewed its leaf and found their vigor restored. Digitalis extract was well know to those people.

He had taken samples and other plants to bring back to Oxford to study. But he had worked there too long, and the passes had become impassable with snow. He had to remain there during the winter with those hospitable people and his guide. It was not until summer that he could leave.

There followed a long and difficult trek to Calcutta. On board ship the accommodations had not been comfortable, either. It was an old freighter which had been on an exploring mission in the South Atlantic, around Cape Horn, and across the Pacific. The crew had been at sea for two years and were bored and boisterous, but on board was an exploring scientist with whom he shared his findings and received in turn information about South America and the Pacific Islands.

Their conversation went on endlessly as they sipped the wine and basked in genial conversation. "I'm so proud of you, Father. You have sacrificed and endured much in order to bring knowledge of faraway lands home to our country."

"I'm proud of you too, son. You have endured much also and survived it with your personality intact."

"So all's well that ends well," James said blissfully.

"It's not ended yet. Now I'm going to track down the wicked captain who did this to you and was responsible for your mother's untimely death. When I see justice done, then it will have ended."

Taken aback, James looked up to see Tom who had come to remove the tableware, standing at his father's elbow, perturbed and about to speak. James frowned and shook his head in a strong message for Tom to hold his tongue. To his father, he said, "Oh, it's been so long ago. That small ship is likely to be out of service by now and the captain no longer at sea."

"Still, there are registries kept from year to year. There should be some record of their whereabouts."

"Why don't we take a walk around my farm? It's still planting season. You can advise me."

After his father had stepped out into the late afternoon sunshine, James turned to Tom. "Listen, you are not to say anything to my father about our past association."

"But . . ."

"I mean it, and I really do insist on instant obedience this time." With that , he went out to join his father.

The very eventful day came to an end. Tom had brought one of the pallets to the cabin and banked the fire for the night. At James's insistence, his father accepted the bed, while he himself lay on the pallet, relating how he and George had built the cabin one summer. It was midnight before they slept.

Had the cock not been crowing so lustily, James might have slept until broad daylight, but in his half-awakened state it came to him that Tom had not occupied the loft during the night. He remembered Tom's look of concern. Tom's extra set of clothes that had hung on the peg were gone. Quietly, James slipped outside.

Approaching the shed, he saw the door open and a fire glowing. When his shoes crunched the gravel by the door, he heard Becky's insistent voice and noted that she knelt in front of the fire basin with her back to the door as she prepared to heat water.

"Tom, we have to talk," she said. "I suppose you think of me as a silly young girl, but if you would be patient with me, I know we could be happy. What good is there in your spending a miserable night outside, huddled in all your clothes in the hay, while I am in here miserable and lonely? We are legally married. Why can't we live like it? If there are problems we could talk them out. Please, Tom, don't walk away from me again," she pleaded.

James did walk away, without a word. Where was Tom? Amid the sounds of the awakening woods, he detected the thudding of an axe and followed it to the clearing where they had worked yesterday. He saw Tom swinging furiously at the tree trunk repeatedly, then stop to rest on a stump with his head in his hands, his shoulders heaving with sighs.

At the touch of James's hand on his shoulder, Tom looked up and the sighs became sobs. "Let me try to help," James urged.

"You said I could be an honorable man, but my past will never let me. I am still a fraud—to your father, to Becky, and surely to God."

"To my father? He has had all the emotional upheaval he can handle for a while. Give him time. Then you can make peace with him. Right now, I fear that he would do something he would later regret. We must protect him from that.

"To God? None of us can ever compensate God to make up for past sins. To be acceptable to God, we must accept Him at his word. He loved us so much that He sent his only Son into our world to be our substitute and bear the punishment for our sins. He has returned to heaven to guide us as we live and to receive us to himself when we die. No amount of self-torture can give you peace. You would always wonder if you had done enough. Just call on God's mercy and accept His complete forgiveness. Jesus Christ already earned it for you. That's the only kind of righteousness that counts before God."

"I've been trying to understand that, but just when I think I believe it, I have doubts that it is really for someone like me. Can I ever be sure?" Tom asked earnestly.

They knelt together in the morning mist, letting God's Spirit bring pardon and healing. They rose as Christian brothers, united as members of God's family.

Walking back to the shed, James continued, "Now as to your wife, here is something else you need to hear."

Repeating Becky's words brought exclamations of pleasure mixed with concern. "Do you think she realizes what she is saying? Has she thought of the consequences?" Tom asked with mounting excitement.

"That's something you two will have to talk about. Here's an idea. Father and I will spend the day with Farlands. Becky will be serving him tea about now, and I will join him. You go to the shed, get out of these sweaty clothes, wash up and relax. It's a wonder that you haven't caught a cold. Take the day off, both of you. Becky thinks that it was you who walked away from her this morning, so you have some explaining to do."

The hours at Farlands were most pleasant, but James remembered that Sarah had not even heard the news yet. The past twenty-four hours had been fraught with emotion and reminiscing, but now he was eager to bring his two most loved ones together.

He left his father regaling his hosts with accounts of his adventures, borrowed a horse, and raced to her house. As he dismounted, Sarah came out of the house and into his arms. "Are you trying to fulfill my fantasy?" she asked.

"Yes, yes, with a fulfillment of my own fantasy," and he began to relate as fast as the words would allow the happenings of the past day.

"Oh Dearest, I want to meet him right now. Let me ride back with you." First they would go by her father's office and then out to Farlands.

Mr. Herndon rejoiced with them, adding, "Remember, tomorrow in church your bans are to be published. I planned to ask you to sit with us, James. Your father is included, too. Will you bring him in for his luggage today? Please, have him stop by here."

As they sped off together, Sarah wanted to know all about the events that had brought his father. James laughed at her eagerness.

"Look, we talked all afternoon and most of the night. It will take months to hear all he has to tell."

Sarah was impressed but not cowed by the stately gentleman whose eyes searched hers before he gallantly kissed the hand of his future daughter-in-law. The well-groomed beard, worn boldly though it was the current style to be clean-shaven, made him look distinguished and yet his amiable demeanor put her at ease. She sensed that she had met his approval also, when he escorted her to a chair and, seating himself nearby, began an easy conversation. Watching them, James reckoned that no man alive was as blessed as he.

Elizabeth broke in later with, "Say, don't we need to be talking about the wedding. It's only three weeks away, you know."

"Yes," James conceded, "but what more is there to do?"

When the women protested emphatically that there were still many details to consider, James shrugged. "I guess I've concentrated on getting a home and farm ready for after the wedding and haven't thought much about the ceremony itself."

"That's all right, James," said his father. "Women don't even feel married unless they've made it complicated."

"From what my friends have told me, it's usually the parents that make it complicated," Sarah retorted.

"You are right," he agreed, "except in my case. I seem to have arrived after everything was settled, and that's fine with me."

"Don't let that bother you," George chimed in. "As the attendants, we offered to have the reception here, but no—Sarah has figured out how she can be the bride and the hostess all in one. She wants it to be at her own father's house."

"Then it's up to us to help her as much as she will let us. Let me know how I can help, Sarah." She answered him with her best smile, and with Elizabeth, retired to another room for more woman talk. They were both charmed by their new acquaintance who had brought with him such grace and good humor.

Left to themselves, the men made plans, too. "I really must get to the shipping office. My loads should be ready for pick up. I need to return the horse I rented."

"I'll send the carriage with you, and a wagon if you need it. We are counting on your staying with us until the wedding, so that this love-sick bridegroom can get something done beside talk and dream," George offered.

"Thank you very much. You have truly been a friend to James, and now to me," Dr. Bankstone stated. "I wish I could have met your father. He must have been a most kind, generous, and capable man."

"He always hoped to be able to meet you. He said you must be a special person to have shaped James's character."

"His mother gets credit for that." The silence that followed was filled with memories of departed loved ones.

The next morning, as James and Sarah sat in the pew with their fathers and heard their marriage bans publicly announced, they felt an outpouring of blessing in their lives together. Devout Christians, trained since childhood in the disciplines of the church, they were inspired by the liturgy, Scripture reading, and the sermon. Songs of faith and praise came naturally and brought peace, hope, and strength.

For Tom and Becky, it did not come so readily. They had visited the revival again and were moved by the simple, clear, challenging message. They had heard also of conflict developing between the established church and the revivalists. The label "Separatists" was being applied to those who had started out to invigorate those churches that had bogged down in dull ritualism. The dissension was disturbing. "We must ask the master about this," Tom said. "He must not find that we are doing this behind his back."

James pondered their question. "You say that you both felt closer to God at the revival? You felt a greater joy and peace during their service? You found the teaching more clear and understandable?" Tom and Becky were nodding assent.

James remembered the Tornsons, so uncomfortable in his church, yet eager to be re-associated with their own. Religious liberty was a reason for which some had left their fatherland, but in some places it was not found in America either. That would have to change if this were to be a free land. He hoped it would soon become a reality.

"Feelings are good if based on the truth. Our feelings can change, but the great truths of scripture don't. It is important that your faith is your very own, and it's important that you continue learning more and more about God's word also." Memories of his confirmation instructions in Oxford came back to James. "You are free to worship wherever you choose, but we will continue to read scripture here at home. If ever you hear something that doesn't agree with that, then we need to discuss it."

The answer relieved Tom. It left James wondering why there was not a systematic form of instruction being done in his church for those seeking answers and for the children. He would have to talk with his future father-in-law about that.

Walter Herndon and James Bankstone, Sr. enjoyed each other's company more and more. "You surely don't intend to return to England now that you have finally been reunited with your son, do you?" Mr. Herndon asked.

"I am really still very undecided. Maybe I am waiting for a revelation. The notes I turned over to the faculty at Oxford will have been either published and entered in the Radcliffe Library of Science, or ignored and discarded by now."

"We would certainly be pleased to have you remain in Richmond. My newspaper's readership would double and more if you would supply us with an account of your adventures each week. We do not get much news of a global nature, and I'm sure it would be most interesting."

"Really? I hadn't thought of that possibility. I suppose I could publish my findings here, if not there, in a less academic vein."

"That's exactly right, and your personal experiences would make them very well accepted. Further, since you have expressed some interest in that proposition, I have another one for you. I have been dreading being alone in this big house. Sarah and James are determined to live on their land at this time. Would you consider sharing the house with me?"

Pleased and flattered by the offer, Dr. Bankstone thought it over briefly and then answered, "I'd like that very much. Tell me how to share the expenses and services with you."

The wedding day came and passed as joyously as the previous month had. Getting all the inhabitants moved into their respective dwellings was an adventure in itself. Sarah's furniture, handwork, and household equipment together with the pieces that James had bought made the little bungalow seem like a palace for the newlyweds, but it was love that made the home.

Back in the cabin, Tom's clothes again hung at the side of the fireplace. Becky's hung at the other side. The days were filled with hard work, good health, and wholesome satisfaction.

As the editor had predicted, Dr. Bankstone's articles were received with enthusiasm. He was asked to speak at public gatherings and to consult with planters.

One day Dr. Bankstone received a letter which he shared with his friend. Mr. Herndon was thrilled. "What a story this will be! Instead of your column this week, let me publish this letter." When the other hesitated, the editor urged, "Let's do it for James and Sarah."

So it was that the next issue of the newspaper contained the announcement, "Dr. Bankstone's column does not appear today so that we may bring you this information contained in a letter received by him two days ago. It is post-marked at Oxford

University and reads in part as follows: 'My esteemed colleague, you should have been here yesterday. The campus was abuzz with the arrival of Sir Henry Pelham, our prime minister. He had heard of your discoveries and perused your records with great interest. He was especially absorbed in your account of Tibet. I think he already envisions an expansion of our trade, based in India.

'You may have heard that over the years our prime ministers have come under attack from political enemies. It would be impossible to surmise how long this one may still have influence with the king. His Majesty, King George II, has taken the unusual step of personally leading British forces to defend his ancestral home at Hanover. There seems to be no end to the wars we are constantly fighting. I wish that our considerable energy could be vested in peaceful pursuits more beneficial to mankind.

'Perhaps, that is what our prime minister also had in mind. On leaving the university, he announced that he would nominate you for honorary knighthood.

'Of course, we are mightily pleased. However, I cannot assure you that it will ever come to pass since the government seems caught up in so much wrangling and so many diversions. We all extend our congratulations, and say that we would be happy to address you as Sir James Bankstone. If there is any further word, I will write you immediately.'

"This newspaper adds its congratulations also."

Nathan, who had managed the Gilroy Quality Printing Establishment quite efficiently since his uncle's early demise, nearly fell off his stool as he began to set type for that issue of the newspaper. James had never mentioned his father in their conversations. The two young men had drifted apart in the past few years, but he would certainly look up his former co-worker and express his congratulations on his marriage, and now on having a famous father.

James and Sarah were delighted with the news, naturally. They were amused to note that people who had ignored James in the past, now wanted to make his acquaintance. Sarah put the fame into perspective when she told James, "I want you to remember that I loved you long before all this became known."

"That's what makes your love so precious to me," he replied.

XIII

Reconciliation and Resolution

Three years have passed. Dr. Bankstone, still afflicted with wanderlust, has traveled extensively throughout the colonies finding much to interest him in the wide variety of climate and plant life along the Atlantic seaboard. He has crossed the Blue Ridge and observed the farming settlements of the German, Swedish, and Scottish immigrants. He marveled at the vastness of the unexplored continent beyond. Still, in his less adventurous moments, he longs for the academic life of the University. Nothing further has been heard from his records of exploration of the Asian continent, but a portion of his report has continued weekly in the Richmond newspaper. A trip back to England has become more appealing, but he doesn't want to go back empty-handed.

One day, he asked James, "Would you spare me a small plot for an experimental garden and also a few days of your good man, Tom?"

"Of course. What are you up to now?"

"I've been urging planters to grow more peanuts instead of the tobacco which depletes the soil so badly. Now I want to find out what it does to people. It's not fit for digestion, yet people consume much of it through their lungs. I've seen other plants smoked in Asia, and they had an immediate, often harmful effect. Seemingly, tobacco has no such effect, but those who use it often do not seem able to give it up easily. I know that opium is in the poppy, but what is in tobacco?"

With Tom's help, Dr. Bankstone spaded up an area of virgin soil and planted it with seed from North Carolina. "People tell me that the tobacco grown there tastes different than that grown here," was the botanist's observation.

"People also say that tobacco grown in old soil tastes different than if grown in virgin soil," Tom added.

"Really? Well, the plant must take up the chemical from the soil to give the different tastes. I must take some from here also."

Tom was only mildly interested in the experiment. His chief interest was their two year old son, John, who now wanted to follow his "Da" everywhere. Tom's love for the boy was fierce since it represented a bond missed in his own childhood. Becky was happy to have Johnny out from under foot as she continued her busy domestic duties, but the sight of the two of them walking hand in hand across the fields brought a lump of pleasure to her throat.

Dr. Bankstone, too, enjoyed the boy and often brought him a sweet biscuit that Jenny had baked for tea. Becky had remonstrated that he was spoiling the boy, but Dr. Bankstone said, "Let me get practiced for spoiling my own grandchild. It's a long time until October. Then, he, or she, won't know me for several months. Becky knew that James and Sarah eagerly anticipated their firstborn.

School had been in session only a few weeks when Mr. Jones suffered apoplexy and was unable to teach. George had now taken his father's position on the council for the preparatory school. He informed James, "We have unanimously decided to offer you the position of temporary schoolmaster. You would be doing all of us a tremendous service to accept."

"You always did know how to word a request in such a way that I could hardly refuse," James answered.

"Good! Then it's settled. I'll tell the council that you will take over next Monday."

"Wait a minute! Did I say yes?"

"I'm certain you did. I'll send a horse over tomorrow for you to keep, and you can ride over to the school to see what's to be done." Sometimes George could be downright imperious, but always generous, and he did remember that James had told the judge that he might like to teach.

Pleased, but somewhat overwhelmed, James told Sarah who was happy and supportive. James would be gone from home for most of the day, but Dr. Bankstone was spending more time there keeping watch over his plants. Elizabeth urged Sarah to stay with her and let Callie care for her, but Sarah assured her friend that she would be all right with Becky standing by, and she wanted the baby born in their own house.

"Tom," Dr. Bankstone said one day, "we must make a drying shed." Stakes were put in the ground. A roof was constructed to keep out the rain, and a long open rack to lay the tobacco leaves on, with a shallow trench for the slow fire underneath was built. It was the way tobacco was dried in small operations, and it was ready for the crop now ripening in the small experimental plot.

Tom needed to spend more time now harvesting corn and sorghum. Becky was busy drying apples, their first good crop from their new trees. There were pumpkins and squash to bring in, and root crops to pull up and store. Johnny preferred to tag along with Dr. Bankstone since all the other adults were running hither and yon, telling him to stay away from their tools. Sarah was glad to have the elder Bankstone nearby.

With a vague sense of uneasiness, Tom watched his son toddling after James's father, wishing that he could have made peace with him before now. Nearly every day when Tom came home from the field, he found the two of them under the shed or sitting near it in a companionable pose. Seeing him approach, Dr. Bankstone called out, "We are nearly ready to finish this. The tobacco is very dry, but I want it so dry that it turns to powder in my hand. Then I'll be sure it will be well preserved when I take it to the laboratory at Oxford, where we'll see if we can analyze it without any contaminant."

Tom asked in surprise, "Does my master know you are returning to England?"

"Not yet. He's been very busy with his school, but I am eager to get back to mine, after the baby is born. I have another purpose for getting back while the sailing is reasonably good. This will be my chance to investigate the whereabouts of the renegade captain who brought us so much grief. Someone like that should not be breathing free air and wreaking havoc on innocent children and their families." Tom was stunned into silence.

They were standing under the roof of the drying shed when Dr. Bankstone determined that the leaves were still to moist to crumble. Breaking off a long dry leaf, he placed the tip into the smoking embers to test for moisture before Tom could utter a warning. In an instant the long leaf caught fire, and the flame shot upward to Dr. Bankstone's hand causing him to drop it on the rack of dry hot leaves. Too surprised to act, he felt the flames singe his beard and soar upward to the roof. Tom grabbed him around the neck, forcing him down and away from the flames and pushing him out from under the overhanging roof to the ground.

Returning to retrieve Johnny, he saw the structure collapse a split second before he could reach under the edge. A supporting beam pressed against the ground gave him a handhold for raising the roof. Frantically, his free hand groped for his son and grasped his arm, pulling him out from the burning roof with flames licking at the back of the boy's shirt. Dr. Bankstone shouted, "I'll take him. Your sleeve is on fire." He held the screaming child with its back on the grass to extinguish the flames while Tom did the same with his own arm.

The whole thing had happened in less time than it takes to tell. Tom rushed with Johnny to the bungalow where he knew Becky was cooking supper. She mixed baking soda with water into a paste and laid it over the burned area as Tom held the boy face down on the table. Gradually the pain subsided and so did the screaming. Tom's arm received the same treatment as Sarah talked soothingly to Johnny.

"What is this stuff? It really works," Tom wanted to know.

"My mother's home remedy—which I never got to use on her," Becky said, starting to feel shaken now that the emergency was over.

Humbly, Dr. Bankstone had watched the treatments from the doorway. It was a tremulous household that greeted James's return. His father was embarrassed, but took full blame for the crisis as he related it to James. "Tom had told me that stuff was very dry, but I explained that I wanted it so dry that it would pulverize, so that I could take it to the laboratory pure."

"You were returning to England?"

"Those were my plans. I would have told you soon. I also wanted to look for that evil captain," his father explained.

"You told Tom that?" James asked specifically.

"Yes, just before the fire broke loose. Tom's a good man—very loyal to you. That's why he took such risks for me. He saved my life, and what is so remarkable is that he saved me first and then went after his son. I asked him why, since he could have gotten Johnny out without a scratch. All he said was, 'The flames were closer to you.' It was really a stupid thing I did."

"Let's go over and see how they are doing," James said, putting his book satchel on the desk and taking from it an old folded paper.

They met Becky coming back to the bungalow to put supper on the table. They found Tom sitting beside his sleeping son's bed, his hand fondling the auburn curls. He rose to his feet as they entered, but Dr. Bankstone objected. "Please, stay seated and try to be comfortable. Are you in much pain?"

"No, sir. Becky's remedy relieved the burning, and I don't even see any blisters. He's not so lucky. Where the pole lay on him, the burn is deep."

"I don't know how to thank you. If there is any way I can repay you, I want you to tell me."

Tom's gaze shifted to James who said, "Father tells me he was planning to go back to England—with a two-fold purpose."

"Yes, I know," Tom replied in a voice so low he was scarcely heard.

"Father, I think we should sit down. I believe Tom has something to tell you," James said.

Tom noted the old paper of indenture James held, and nodded. "What you can do for me will save my life," he began, and recounted the events that had brought himself and James together, and their meeting again which was also fraught with conflict until resolved by pardon and love. "You should know as well, how I misused your name in all this. Master has the contract I forced him to sign on pain of further branding."

"Branding?" the question came explosively.

James showed his father the scars and handed him the paper to read. Changing emotions registered in Dr. Bankstone's face. He had chastised himself repeatedly for leaving his son alone, but the paper labeled him a violent and abusive father. How ironic! Now before him was the real tormentor of them all.

Tom's chin trembled as he looked down on his precious son. "I deserve the scars, but not my son." A leaden silence followed. "I've caused so much pain. I know how I would feel if it had been my son. Please, try to forgive me like your son and God have done." He sank to his knees in remorse.

Dr. Bankstone spoke at last, "This . . . is . . . too much," and strode out of the cabin.

"He'll be all right. We will all be all right. I'm proud of you, Tom," James said, rising to follow his father.

They talked a long time. James explained the conditions of Tom's childhood. "He found me where he himself had stood some twelve years earlier. He had been in rags, barefoot, and nearly starved when he went begging to the former captain of that ship to take him on as a cabin boy. I was well-dressed and cared for—only amusing myself with dreams of sea travel. The galling unfairness of life infuriated him. Having tasted that myself, I can understand. He's a changed man . . . and he saved your life."

Finally James said, "It's nearly sunset. We are told not to let the sun go down on our wrath." His father walked slowly back to the cabin. Words would not come, but he extended his hand. Tom took it gratefully, but looked for more of an answer in the eyes that would not meet his.

"He'll be back," James promised. "He said that there's no reason for him to go back to England now."

With Walter Herndon, Dr. Bankstone was able to discuss the day's discoveries. "Did you know about this?"

"No. James kept it very quiet. Once he told me that he had been kidnapped. He wanted me to understand that he came from a good family. Judge Farland had already told me of his efforts to find you. I understand that James broke down when the judge received a letter stating that your wife had died. His hopes were very faint at the time of ever seeing you again."

"He has suffered much more than I, but he forgives completely. I know I must, but how can I? When I think of my dear wife dying in grief, my years of self-accusation. . ."

Walter Herndon looked at him with affection. "Friend, I could quote you Matthew 18: 21-35, but why don't you read it for yourself. You will know what to do."

Dr. Bankstone lay awake on his bed. There were so many adventures to be had in life, but in times of soul-searching, they all paled compared to the prospect of facing one's Maker. It had been a long time since he had been as honest with himself as Tom was with him earlier. He recalled the jealousies among the faculty he had participated in; the years in India among the obsequious low-caste servants—he had not been cruel, but not considerate either; the woman in Tibet who had nursed him through a bout of malaria left over from India—she had shared his bed in the winter in the mode of native hospitality, and then he had simply walked away in the spring. He had drifted from his own spiritual moorings into those of other cultures, where he had shared their fallacies instead of bringing them the word of the Almighty. "Forgive me, too, Lord," he prayed, "and help me."

With peace came sleep. The will and the words to heal the wound that had festered so long were there for him when he met Tom in the morning.

James was realizing the problems of the classroom from a different angle. Juggling challenges for those who didn't care to learn, those who could not learn without extra attention, and those who wanted to learn more than he had prepared was making it necessary to spend hours of preparation by candlelight. It also brought a new respect for Nigel Jones. From George, he learned that his former teacher was now bedridden, paralyzed on one side, and speaking only with difficulty. Having no relative or family around, with only a daytime attendant to care for his hygiene and nutritional needs, must be depressing.

James didn't know how he would be received, but felt a visit would be good for both of them. The attendant went to announce his arrival and spent some time getting Mr. Jones presentable before ushering James into the old schoolmaster's presence. As he neared the bed, Mr. Jones greeted him somberly, "Ecce helluo librorum." (Behold the bookworm.)

James chuckled. Yes, he had been a bookworm and had probably annoyed the teacher more than once with his engrossed oblivion to his surroundings. Seeing him in such an obvious attempt at stateliness, James replied, "Ecce otium cum dignitate." (Behold ease with dignity.)

That brought a crooked smile and an invitation to be seated. "Thank you for seeing me today. I need your advice on several matters," James began.

Mr. Jones could speak only slowly and often unclearly. James forced himself to wait and not to press for details. In less than half an hour, it was plain to see that the schoolmaster was tiring. "It was very kind of you to help me. I really must be going. I hope that you will soon be feeling better."

He took the good left hand in both of his and felt how weak it was. "Glad you came; come again. Good-bye," Mr. Jones said.

The next afternoon George stopped him on the way home. "We have just buried Nigel Jones. We heard that you were the last of his former students to see him alive. A tombstone has been ordered. Do you have any idea for an inscription?"

James was surprised to find himself so moved, and felt George look at him quizzically. "Yes," he answered. "'Here lies Nigel Jones, a teacher to the end. Sit tibi terra levis.'"

"He always did like his Latin phrases. What does it mean?"

"May the earth lie lightly on thee."

"That's good," said George as he wrote it down.

Elizabeth called to him from the veranda. She expressed her concern that Sarah would be giving birth with so little help standing by. "Please, talk to her about coming here where there are more of us to help. I believe she thinks she would be disloyal to have the baby anywhere but at your house."

Filled with deep tenderness for the woman who had given him so much, he rushed home. He had been so preoccupied that he hadn't realized that her waiting time was nearly over.

She did not greet him at the door, and when he entered the bungalow, he knew why. Lying on the bed, breathing deeply and trying not to show fear of the labor pains that seized her rhythmically, she greeted him with tearful relief. "They started so quickly. Becky has gone to get Tom to go for help. She's been so wonderful and calm, but I dreaded being alone after she left," Sarah sobbed.

Thoroughly shaken, James fumbled with the bed linen. "Oh my darling, I am so sorry I didn't make this easier for you."

Tom and Becky were both running toward the house now. "Take the horse and get Callie," James shouted, and Tom sped away.

Becky was the essence of calm again. "She'll be here very soon. We could probably do this all by ourselves, but Callie is such a comfort to have around."

"Where did you get all this maturity?" James wondered aloud.

"Nothing like experience," she retorted, and reached for Sarah's hand as another contraction bore the precious contents of her womb a bit closer to the outside world.

Becky had been keeping a clean pot with water on hand. Now she asked James to build up the fire and swing the pot in place. She went to the wooden chest and took out the tiny clothes she and Sarah had been sewing. "We'll soon see if these fit," she said cheerily, holding them up so Sarah could see. In spite of her discomfort, Sarah nodded and smiled, relaxing during the respite between birth pains.

When Callie arrived, Becky said, "It's time for you fellows to get out," and firmly motioned them to the door. James remembered walking with Tom while the latter agonized through Becky's delivery. Now, he was experiencing first hand the sweet agony of the loving expectant father.

It seemed forever before they heard the cry of the new-born girlchild who continued to wail lustily. "Sounds healthy," Tom commented, but James was already halfway to the door. He was vaguely aware of Elizabeth arriving on horseback, followed by George. Greeting them would have to wait.

He knelt at the bedside and kissed his wife's moist forehead. Callie placed a wriggling, wrinkled bundle in her arms. "She is lovely, isn't she?" Sarah said, beaming.

"*You* are lovely. She is . . . red."

The women hooted. "They're all like that at first," Becky said. "They are not born with lovely brown curls, you know."

Recovering quickly, James stated, "Of course, she's lovely. She's just not a miniature Sarah, yet. When may I hold her?"

"Every time she cries," Becky replied.

Callie was more gentle with his new fatherhood. "You can hold her now if you wish."

James picked up the wee thing who opened her mouth in a wide yawn and promptly fell asleep. The deep affirmation of parenthood claimed him. Sarah, watching them with shining eyes, shared their moment of bonding. "Thank you, my beloved," he whispered for her ears alone.

"Well, I see you survived," George chortled in mock condescension. "Congratulations!"

"Naturally. After nursing the two of you men through your crises, I was prepared . . . not at all." It was no time for nonchalance.

Elizabeth sat on the bed chatting excitedly as she and Sarah already compared mothering experiences. Johnny was allowed a peek at the new baby, and then Callie said that Sarah needed to rest and they would all do well to leave.

She was so right. While her baby was being bathed, Sarah asked numerous questions and wanted to see her toes and straight active legs, but by the time the baby was wrapped again in a blanket, the new mother was sleeping blissfully.

"Tom, will you make one more ride for me? Tell those two gentlemen living on Spruce Street that they have a brand new granddaughter."

Watching Tom ride away, Elizabeth commented, "She's a lucky little girl to have two resident grandfathers." She had hoped that her parents would be brave enough to make the journey to visit them, but she doubted that they were adventurous enough for that.

XIV

Not So Lonesome

James found that teaching was the most demanding work he had ever done. Preparing to teach the academics took more hours than he had anticipated. The discussions that ensued often destroyed his lesson schedule. A history lesson would lead into a debate on moral values; geography was followed by further questions from those who yearned to broaden their horizons; and mathematics brought up possibilities he hadn't defined. He wondered what Nigel Jones, or even the Education Council, would think if they knew of the distractions he tolerated in the classroom. The school term was nearly over. A qualified instructor would be brought in soon and repair the damage he had done, he thought.

He regretted also that he spent so much of the day away from Sarah and little Josephine. When riding home, he frequently met Elizabeth riding back to her house with Katherine, who was now four years old and full of vitality and curiosity. Sarah would relate what

Josie and Kitty had done during their visits. It was the way of women to turn proper names into endearing pet names, he surmised.

One spring day was made even more distracting when George came to visit the school. After the students left, he explained. "I was given the duty of visiting the school. If everything was proceeding smoothly, I was to offer you this contract as permanent headmaster of Jones Memorial Preparatory School. I truly hope you will accept."

"That would solve your problem nicely, wouldn't it?"

"Well, yes, it would, but it's a good opportunity for you, too, isn't it?" George answered, a bit taken aback.

"An opportunity to be inadequate. I'm not educated to be a headmaster and you know it. I've tried to do my best, but I'm not satisfied with the results. My years of being your servant have conditioned me to do whatever you ask, but it's not fair to the students that I should be used as a convenience for the Education Council." James was himself amazed at the tension in his insecurity.

Astounded, George tried to understand his friend's feelings. "Look," he began hesitantly, "if I've seemed overbearing about this, I apologize. I haven't learned to always think before I speak. It really hurts to know that you feel I've been using you as a convenience. Can't you give me credit for having changed since our first month together? Ever since then I've thought of you as a friend, not a servant; now as a brother. I should have divided the estate equally with you, because without *you* . . . I would have come home to nothing."

"No. Don't be ridiculous," James protested. "I'm not envious of your wealth. Maybe it's my lack of formal education that has given me feelings of inferiority."

"I'm afraid you don't realize your own worth. With equal opportunity you would have quite surpassed me. Your parentage is at least equal to mine. Your father should have been knighted. You should have had access to a college education. But even with things as they are at the moment, you don't realize what you have meant to this school. You have a real talent for bringing out the best in the students. The enrollment for next year has increased because of your reputation. James, don't let your lack of a formal education excuse you from using your talent. The Council has asked me to draw up plans for a new and larger building. Although we acknowledge that the most important building going on here is in the minds of these students. Today I found myself wishing that you had been my teacher. In a way, I guess you were." George spoke sincerely.

"Maybe it's my turn to apologize. I do appreciate the encouragement. I'll admit that I enjoy the challenge of teaching, and I would like for Sarah to be able to look forward to an an easier life than that of a pioneer," James said, smiling faintly. "She used to enjoy helping her father with the newspaper, but now she hardly ever gets into town during the week. At least my teacher's salary has helped us buy a few extras."

"Take a look at that contract. You haven't seen the salary that's offered now. That should take care of your feelings of inferiority," George remarked.

James could not have asked for better terms. He read over the contract a second time. "You would offer this to a teacher who can't even keep his class on schedule, or stick to a subject? It must have been my friend in high places that caused this."

"I only voted with the majority. Will you please stop putting yourself down? It's precisely because you make education a process for life that you have so much success. Don't you remember how you got me interested in architecture when I thought that all I could do was sketch buildings? You made it real for me," George declared. "Why not talk to your father about what it might take to get certified?"

"I don't know how much longer he'll be here. I think he is getting restless to get into something major. He may know how someone my age could still get a formal education."

They had established a tradition of having the grandfathers come to dinner on Friday. In return, the little family went to the Herndon home for dinner on Sunday after church. These times were anticipated eagerly. Happy to be home for the week-end, James savored the aromas of cooking as he laid his books on the desk. He would talk with his father this evening about the possibility of his becoming a full-fledged educator.

Sarah was busily preparing vegetables. "Dear, will you please fetch a pail of water. I'll need more for cooking and later for washing up." Cheerfully, he did so. "Where is Becky?" he asked when he returned from the new well which the women called 'the wife saver.'

"She has not been feeling well for about a month and today was especially rough. I told her to stay in bed. Did you know that she is expecting another baby?"

"No. When?"

"In about five months. I should have suspected it earlier. When Josie was born and Elizabeth was visiting, Elizabeth asked Callie if it is easier the second time, and Becky said, 'I'll let you know.' I was too wrapped up in my own life just then, and I'm afraid I haven't been as considerate as I might have been."

"That presents another factor. In five months her indenture will have been completed. There will have to be some changes."

"What do you mean? Surely she wouldn't be leaving when Tom still has two more years."

"Oh no, of course not. There need to be different arrangements made, though, as to compensation. Here, let me lift that heavy pot for you."

When questioned, Dr. Bankstone answered, "If we were in England, I could tell you how to get certified. If teaching is what you want to do, I'm sure there is a way for you to feel comfortable in that position." Then the talk turned to Josie's latest accomplishment, and not much more was said on the subject.

It was less than a week later when Dr. Bankstone made an unscheduled visit to the bungalow. "I've been to Williamsburg. You can sit for an oral examination by a panel of professors at the college in June. If the results are favorable, you will be offered a written examination in July. If you are successful in that, you will receive certification as a Preparatory School Master. If you fail the oral examination, you will be given a course of study to pursue until you are able to pass it. Here is a list of books you would do well to study."

Thrilled, James scanned the list. "Several of these are in the judge's library. I'm sure I could borrow them."

His father continued, "I'll help you as much as I can, that is, until July. Then I'll be moving."

"You are going back to England?" James asked sadly.

"No, I am moving to Williamsburg. I have been offered a position at the college, to teach science and do agriculture research. It's a great opportunity, and I've already accepted. I'll not even be daunted by all those clergymen on the faculty."

"This is such exciting news! I'm happy for you . . . and for me. Stay for dinner and tell us more."

"Thank you, no. Walter and I have quite a lot to talk over. We won't be out tomorrow, either. See you Sunday."

An hour or so in the evenings and on Saturdays was the only time James could spend farming. The wheat had sprouted well and stood tall, straight, and dense. It was relatively weed-free and would easily lend itself to the wide swoops of the scythe when ripe. The corn, planted in hills, needed weeding, and that could be a boring task. Tom was always glad when James joined him with a hoe, and they could talk as they worked. Dr. Bankstone's experimental plot was now sown to peanuts which he checked regularly. Becky's garden had become a miniature farm with its sections of sweet potatoes, white potatoes, and vegetables of all kinds. James had told Tom to take time to help her care for it, until she felt able to resume. The shed now held a cow and a yearling calf. There were a dozen hens and numerous half-grown chickens that would soon make a delicious addition to the menu.

Sarah had taught James to shoot, and he had successfully bagged a deer during the winter. Wild turkeys lurked in the wooded patches. George invited James for hunting every fall. There was no lack of food for the table, James thought, as he worked his hoe around the stalks of corn. The salary he was contemplating accepting would make it possible to acquire more comforts. Yes, he would do it.

"The grandfathers won't be here for dinner this evening, so we'll be eating together. We need to talk, Tom," James said. "Let's put up our hoes early."

With supper ended and dishes cleared away, it was discussion time. "Becky, it's good to see you able to eat again. I hope you are feeling much better," James began.

"It always gets better after the evening meal—morning sickness that lasts all day—it will soon pass." She was not given to complaining.

"You will be giving birth about the time your indentures are completed. Have you given any thought to what you want to do when you are free of your contract?" James asked.

"My only plan is to stay with my husband for life."

"I thought as much and am glad to hear you say it."

"That troubles me, sir. I have sworn to serve you for life and that is still my intention," Tom said.

"But that is not a reason for Becky to give up her freedom. Freedom is very precious," James stated emphatically.

Tom and Becky looked at each other uneasily. "We hoped that you would find a solution."

"I'm sure there is a solution to be found. For now, I want you to know that I'll arrange for Callie to help you whether your baby is born before or after your indentures are completed."

"Tom," he continued, "for the next two months I'll be spending a lot of time studying. I have a chance to get my schoolmaster certification, and I'm going to give it my best effort. That means that most of running the farm will be up to you with very little help from me. It won't be an easy summer, but we'll all have to do our best." He pushed his chair back from the table, and to Sarah's surprise, announced, "While you finish up here, Sarah and I are going to take a walk."

The time had come to tell Sarah about his experiences with Tom and how it happened that Becky arrived. Sarah knew that the scars on his back had been caused by his kidnapper and had questioned no further. He had seen her puzzled look when Tom spoke of lifelong servitude. More questions would surface.

"Am I the last one to know all this?" she asked after hearing the amazing story.

"George knew because Tom told him after the incident with the knife, but I asked him for secrecy until we would see what would come of it. I don't think he has told Elizabeth. I didn't tell you because I didn't want you to feel uncomfortable around him. Tom confessed to Father after the fire when he wanted to reward Tom for saving him. Tom asked for his forgiveness instead."

"I can hardly believe that our Tom could do such a thing."

"It wasn't our Tom. It was the old Tom."

She nodded. "Does Becky know?"

"I think so. Tom is very protective of women. It was men, especially rich ones who might have abused his mother, that he despised. He loved his mother dearly. I don't know what drove her to prostitution, but he understood that she did what she had to in order to protect him. When the abuse was put on him in order to control her, she sent him away, and he never saw her again. Becky is so grateful to him for saving her from a similar fate that she could overlook his past. I wasn't totally honest with you when I didn't correct your assumption that she was his fiancee coming here to be married to him. Actually, they married as strangers to protect my reputation. That concerned me greatly, but I believe their marriage is working out quite well."

"Yes. She adores him. He's her knight in shining armor. You were wise not to tell me, though, until I learned to value him. I might have scratched his eyes out at that time."

"Yeah, I heard you even came after George once when he was giving me a hard time in school." They could laugh now at the recollection.

"I loved you then already; but Dearest, I love you even more now. You are even more noble than I thought."

"Sweetheart, you have brought me so much tenderness, confidence, and happiness. I love you more every day. You are truly a helpmate from God, and an answer to prayer."

Sunday at the Herndon house pulsated with exciting discussion. Dr. Bankstone's post at the college meant more to him than the proposed knighthood which had never materialized. Walter Herndon wanted to be a part of the adventure. "I'm going to Williamsburg with him for a few days. I haven't visited there in a long time. James, feel free to use my library to prepare for your examination. Sarah, please look over the script for the newspaper if I'm not back in time. I'll tell the writers that you represent me."

Riding back to the bungalow, Sarah commented, "Father will be so lonely again after your father moves away."

They stopped at the Farland house to chat. George graciously urged James to select any books from the study that would be useful to him, adding, "I need to ask a favor of you and Sarah. I will be spending several days a week in Hopewell to supervise building a new church there. I also have a contract for a new courthouse in Hanover County. I hate to leave Elizabeth so long. I wish you and

Sarah would come to see her more often. The total absence of both our families makes her a little homesick. Now she has been having morning sickness, too."

"Well, we know what that means. You are hoping for a George, Jr., I suppose. Congratulations on your business success, too! We should set Callie up in business. Our three households give her plenty of experience to add to her recommendations. Becky will be needing her about the end of October. I hope it's all right with you if I arrange with Callie to help her," James replied.

"Certainly. Callie has become our resident grandmother."

Riding on to their home, Sarah behind James, holding little Josie snugly in her arms, Sarah said, "Elizabeth and I are getting to be more like sisters every day. She shares her mother's wisdom with me. I didn't know how much I was missing."

"I'm glad that Josie has a good mother," James answered. It would be easy and pleasant to honor George's request.

Ten days later, James accompanied his father and father-in-law to the pier. "Take good care of these two," he told the boatmen. He himself would be making the trip in another week to take his oral examination. He and Mr. Herndon would return together. In the meantime, Sarah would look after both households plus checking on the lay-out of the week's newspaper.

She was waiting at the docks as their returning boat was poled up to shore. "Tell me quickly. How did it go?" she asked.

"Apparently well enough. I'm invited back for the written test next month," James announced.

"I knew you would do it. And how did you like Williamsburg, Father?"

"It's a very interesting place, so full of happenings right now. The House of Burgesses fairly throbs with oratory. Some voice strong objections to any ruling from England; others say our future rests with the fatherland. I met the newspaper editor. He is interesting, but very opinionated. Well, here is my carriage. I'll be going."

"It's Friday. Aren't you coming out for dinner?"

"No, thanks. I have had quite enough traveling for one day. But I'll look for you on Sunday."

Sarah told James, "I hate for him to go back to that big house all by himself. Maybe he sensed that we would like to be by ourselves this evening."

"Bless him!" James said, smiling.

The abundant Sunday dinner that Jenny set on the Herndon table took away James's zeal for studying, and he had to fight sleep as he watched Mr. Herndon settle into his comfortable chair. Before long their host would be taking a nap. Today was different, however. Mr. Herndon was full of energy and soon told them that he had news for them.

"Do you remember that I mentioned that I had met the editor in Williamsburg? Well, he wants to retire and return to England. Life in the colony, even in Williamsburg, has never been to his liking. He is putting the paper up for sale, and I made an offer to buy it."

"Father!" Sarah couldn't believe she had heard correctly.

James was no longer sleepy. "What on earth made you do that?"

"I have felt the need for a change for quite some time. One gets stale doing the same thing year after year. After all, you have been changing your lives. James, your father has rented a more than adequate house and has asked me to share it with him if our deal goes through. Being in the capital, I'll have the opportunity to keep my hand on the pulse of government."

"But what about the house? And the newspaper here? It's been your life. You can't just walk away from it?"

"Yes, I can; but I'm hoping that you will consider walking into it. James, you'll be much closer to the school here. We have some good writers on the staff. I've already talked to them. Sarah, you have a gift for knowing what's appropriate and readable. You'll make a fine editor, and you have James to make suggestions like you used to do for me.

It was a lot to absorb at one time. "But you are not sure of securing the purchase, right? Maybe you will still be staying. I just can't picture the house without you in it," she said wistfully.

"That's why I really hope that you will decide to live in it, to keep it in the family. Anyway, think it over, and we'll see what the next few weeks bring." He seemed invigorated.

It took a great deal of time for James to prepare for his written examination. His father had invited all of them to stay with him during the days of tests. It was the only way, he said, that they could all be together for the victory celebration when James would get his certificate.

With such encouragement, James was successful. Triumphantly he declared himself ready for some light-hearted relaxation. "Now we want to see your school, Father."

"Yes, let the celebration begin." They started with a guided tour of the college. Dr. Bankstone already had ideas for its expansion. Law, literature, languages were all right, he declared, but a new country needed the practical science courses, such as engineering, medicine, architecture, and agriculture. "Here, though, is a practical venture that is way past my thinking," he said, laughing. "This building houses our college brewery. No joking."

Walter Herndon, who had not been with them for the tour, met them later that evening. He had his own triumph. "By September 1, the Williamsburg newspaper will be mine. James, I'd like to move here in about four weeks," he told the senior Bankstone.

Sarah thought, . . . and I worried about my poor, old, lonely father. What a busy time it would be for all of them! She would help her father pack and move. James would be preparing for school, but also moving their household to the Herndon home on

Spruce Street. Becky would be gathering in the fall provisions as Tom did the field harvesting. She herself would need to spend time at the newspaper, arranging with her father a distribution of duties for the staff.

XV

The Building Extended

School had gotten well underway. There was a nip of fall in the air. The breeze coming through the open door felt good. The students had gone home. James sat at his desk studying George's plans for a new school building that would include a Franklin stove instead of an open fireplace. Noiselessly, a shadow crossed the desk. He looked up to see that the quiet intruder was Horace Russell, seemingly larger than life, holding a rifle by the barrel with the butt resting on the floor, and carrying a powder horn by a shoulder strap. Was this to be a final confrontation? There seemed to be more curiosity than animosity in his look.

"I heard you were the new schoolmaster. I thought I'd drop by to say 'Hello,'" Horace said a bit uncertainly.

"Have you been hunting?"

"No, sir. A soldier always keeps his rifle with him."

"Soldier? Have you been with Col. Washington?" James asked.

Horace nodded. "Yes, sir, two years."

"How was it?"

"Educational," was Horace's laconic reply.

"How is Bruce?"

"I'm waiting to meet him. His ship is due in tomorrow."

"He went to sea?" James asked, hardly believing his ears.

"Yes, sir." Horace shifted his feet. "I may have to teach him some manners." He was looking keenly for signs of rancor.

"What made you decide to venture out?" James wanted to know.

A pause, and Horace developed a slow grin. "Well, sir, it's like this. We didn't figure you dared to give us a wrong answer a second time." So scantly he referred to their previous confrontations.

James had to grin at that, too. "Your father?" he asked.

"Died two years ago. Well, I've got to be going. We're moving out again next week. Good day, sir."

They shook hands. "Good-bye, Horace. Greet Bruce for me, and take care of yourself."

Horace left as quietly as he had come, leaving James shaking his head in amazement. "People are like clay. We get shaped, re-shaped, and sometimes baked hard," he mused, "but not chip-proof." So ended the last of the insults of his past fourteen years. There would be no more derision from the Russells.

Spring was rolling around again. George and Elizabeth were visiting at the house on Spruce Street. The men were talking on the veranda. "How are things at the farm?" George asked.

"I spent several hours of hard labor out there yesterday and decided that this is the year I'll invest in better equipment. A plow like the one Joe uses would make a big difference. Do you think he has time to make us one?"

"Yes, but have you seen the grain drill? I saw one used on a big farm in England. Now there are some for sale here in Richmond. It makes neat rows, and the weeding is much easier."

James's interest sparked. "We have just gotten a copy of Jethro Tull's *Horse-hoeing Husbandry,* and he mentions that. What I want to know is how one is to raise enough grain to feed the oxen or horses through the winter to pull those implements in the spring and summer."

"Turnips," George said. "That's what a man in England is promoting. They call him 'Turnip Townshend,' but he has a good answer. They grow right up to winter freezing, and the horses love them."

"What a great idea! Hey, you are getting to be a farmer."

"Not really," George protested. "I don't mind reading about it. I just don't like doing it. I'm even thinking of selling off some of the estate. The renters are getting the itch to be owners, and I could use the cash to set up a building business. With their babies coming along, they want their own land. By the way, was that a girl Becky had last fall?"

"No, another boy, and he's growing like a weed."

"Callie told me that you gave her ten pounds for delivering the last three babies at your place."

"Her reputation is growing," James said. "Who knows? She may find one of her children some day and be able to buy his freedom."

"How is Tom doing now that Becky is free?" George asked.

"We worked out a crop-sharing agreement with one third going to Becky. He needs to leave his past behind him and start working toward his family's future, but he still says that he wants to serve for life."

George pondered silently for a few minutes. "Providing for the next generation is a big responsibility, isn't it?"

"George Jr. already has made you think of that, eh?"

"It's not the providing so much as it is the motivating. We've had practice in that already. Remember how you urged me to apply myself? Then I pushed you into your career since you had said once that teaching is what you would like to do some day. I just pushed that day a little closer," George reflected.

"Now Sarah and I are urging you to run for the House of Burgesses, and we have the newspaper to support you."

"Sarah is doing a good job with the newspaper. I noticed that she now lists both your names as editors," George observed.

"She did that to avoid criticism from the folks who think that it's a disgrace for a woman to work at anything that's not domestic. It would be a shame to let that clever mind lie idle. People are still chuckling over her November editorial 'Your Wife Wants a Well for Christmas.' It was her idea to print current trends in agriculture now that Father's travelogue has run out."

"Her clever mind put us to shame a few times in school, I remember," George was smiling with the recollection.

"I used to wonder whether the other three girls in that school were being coy when they didn't answer the questions the boys missed, or if they really didn't know," James said.

"That wasn't Sarah's style. She always did her best."

"Her father treated her like a son; now she's a strong woman."

"Your father really enjoyed presenting the two of you with that fine carriage and harness horse at Christmas," George said.

"We were totally surprised. He said that he regretted not being able to give it as a wedding present. Just having him there was the best wedding present of all. He said he wanted to be sure we had it before another grandchild came along. Can you picture four of us on one horse?" James said with appreciation.

"You are blest to have a living father," George said wistfully.

"Your father would be happy to see your interest in government. How does Elizabeth feel about your standing for election to the House of Burgesses?"

"She is very supportive. It has been good for her to expand her social circles. She's quite a charmer, you know. However, she thinks the emphasis on frivolous fashion is overdone, as I do. Did you hear that perky Mrs. Simpson was ostracized by the ladies of fashion because she dared to wear a hat with a plume? They maintained that such attire was to be reserved for the ladies of high society. Elizabeth told them that if Mrs. Simpson could afford it, she was entitled to wear it. She'll be a voice of moderation and good sense."

"Is she still homesick sometimes?" James asked.

"She hasn't mentioned it. I know she wrote her parents about the boldness of Sarah's father and yours in their new ventures. I am hoping to surprise Elizabeth if I can persuade them to accept the written guarantee for their fare I sent them. She would be ecstatic."

"They would surely be surprised to see how stimulating our life is here," James surmised.

"Ah, yes," George answered. "We're becoming as aristocratic as the upper class in England. Last month a prosperous farmer entered his horse in a race just outside of Williamsburg. He was reprimanded for breaking a rule of etiquette. It seems that horse racing was meant to be only for gentlemen. It reminded me of what my father told me when I said that I wanted to be an architect. He said he was glad that I wanted to be more than a gentleman—the kind who would only take but give nothing back to society. They live only for their entertainment. It must be an empty life without goals."

A comfortable silence ensued. Then George asked, "What was that we used to call ourselves while we built the cabin? 'Builders of the nation' . . . and we're not even a nation, just a string of colonies."

"Builders of the nation." They had said it simultaneously, with an exaggerated intonation, laughing.

They needed not to have laughed. It was a valid assertion. They were exerting influence on many lives. They were building the future of this nation which for most of a century had floundered in exploitive opportunism but was now settling into constructive endeavors.

Ahead lay the country's increasing conflict with King George III. The morality of a revolt, as opposed to allegiance to one's sovereign, just or not, would be vehemently debated. In the end, what God had ordained would come to pass, and He would bring good out of all that conflict. Strong voices opposing slavery and promoting religious liberty would come in the next generation. From the House of Burgesses, the first elected legislative body of the New World, would come the framers of the Declaration of Independence and the Constitution of the United States of America.

Builders of the Nation, we thank you. The job goes on.

The End